T0293005

CREATING GENDER-INCLUSIVE ORGANIZATIONS

EDITED BY
ELLEN ERNST KOSSEK AND KYUNG-HEE LEE

CREATING GENDER-INCLUSIVE ORGANIZATIONS

Lessons from Research and Practice

UNIVERSITY OF TORONTO PRESS
Toronto Buffalo London

ISBN 978-1-4875-0373-4 (cloth)
ISBN 978-1-4875-1861-5 (EPUB)
ISBN 978-1-4875-1860-8 (PDF)

Library and Archives Canada Cataloguing in Publication

Title: Creating gender-inclusive organizations : lessons from research and
practice / edited by Ellen Ernst Kossek and Kyung-Hee Lee.
Names: Kossek, Ellen Ernst, editor. | Lee, Kyung-Hee, 1972– editor.
Description: "This book includes a summary of remarks and essays
by thought leaders who spoke at the inaugural Leadership Excellence
and Gender in Organizations Conference held at Purdue University
organized by the Krannert School of Management and the Susan
Bulkeley Butler Center for Leadership Excellence." – Foreword. |
Includes bibliographical references.
Identifiers: Canadiana (print) 20200152289 | Canadiana (ebook) 20200152335 |
ISBN 9781487503734 | ISBN 9781487503734 (cloth) | ISBN 9781487518608
(PDF) | ISBN 9781487518615 (EPUB)
Subjects: LCSH: Diversity in the workplace. | LCSH: Women – Employment. |
LCSH: Sex role in the work environment. | LCSH: Leadership in women. |
LCSH: Career development.
Classification: LCC HF5549.5.M5 C74 2020 | DDC 658.3008 – dc23

University of Toronto Press acknowledges the financial assistance to its
publishing program of the Canada Council for the Arts and the Ontario Arts
Council, an agency of the Government of Ontario.

 Canada Council   Conseil des Arts
for the Arts   du Canada

 ONTARIO ARTS COUNCIL
CONSEIL DES ARTS DE L'ONTARIO
an Ontario government agency
un organisme du gouvernement de l'Ontario

Funded by the   Financé par le
Government   gouvernement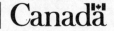
of Canada   du Canada

CONTENTS

FOREWORD

ALYSSA PANITCH

This book includes a summary of remarks and essays by thought leaders who spoke at the inaugural Leadership Excellence and Gender in Organizations Conference held at Purdue University, organized by the Krannert School of Management and the Susan Bulkeley Butler Center for Leadership Excellence. The Susan Bulkeley Butler Center for Leadership Excellence was founded at Purdue in 2004 to be a catalyst for developing women in leadership roles and enhancing an understanding of women and work.

For two days in March 2016, we heard about gender gaps in career equality at the inaugural Leadership Excellence and Gender in Organizations Symposium. We also heard about strategies to promote gender equality, diversity, and career success. We were continuing a journey that began at Purdue eighty years ago. In 1935, Purdue held its first-ever conference on women's careers. We had just over 6,500 students – 986 of them women. At that time, a questionnaire was sent to all Purdue women students asking their opinions about jobs and careers. The person who asked for the survey and who stood before the audience reporting on the results at the conference back then was a faculty member named Amelia Earhart, the first woman aviator to fly across the Atlantic Ocean from America.

A few years earlier, the president of Purdue, Edward C. Elliott, and Amelia had happened to be speaking at the same event in New

York. She had just completed her famous flight across the Atlantic. President Elliott heard her speech and was very impressed with what she had to say about women's roles in the development of aviation. The next day, he was seated next to Amelia at a luncheon, and he discovered that, in his words,

> her primary interest in life was not in this career of adventure upon which she had embarked, but rather in an effort to find and make some addition to the solution of the problem of careers for women. She was interested primarily in the education of women in order to qualify them for their places in the world.

He said it was fate that brought him together with Amelia that day. He made her an offer to come to Purdue and explore what he called "the present wilderness of women's education."

Amelia accepted the offer, and that brings us back to our first-ever conference, which was held in November of 1935 at the Purdue Memorial Union. The theme was "Women's Work and Opportunities."

Amelia reported the results of the questionnaire to her largely female audience:

- 92 percent of all women students who answered the questions planned to work after leaving college.
- 7 percent were undecided.
- Their reasons for seeking employment were:
  - To achieve professional success (to have the mental stimulus of accomplishing something)
  - To attain personal independence
  - Because of economic necessity

However, when they were asked whether women should work after marriage, only 13 percent said yes. The reason for not working was that work would interfere with administering the home.

Here is what Amelia had to say to those young women:

I know it is very hard to look ahead and see yourselves as married women of forty, with your children away at Purdue, your husband busy with his work, and you with no particular interest but the four walls of home. My hope is that those of you who decided so positively that women should under no circumstances work after marriage will not be victims of your present outlook.

Near the end of her speech, Amelia spoke of "the ideal state, i.e., when both husband and wife earn and are jointly responsible for the home (of course, with credit on the ledger for the wife who bears children)." She closed her remarks that day as follows:

Economists sing of the happy days when everyone will work for his or her own living … With the proper distribution of work, the required period for earning the necessities of life would be but a few hours a day, and but six or seven years out of a lifetime … May I hope the career conferences, of which this is the first at Purdue, may do their share in bringing on the ideal state, whatever it may be?

Well, Amelia, we haven't yet reached the "ideal state" you spoke of, but we're closer now than we were eighty years ago. And so, ladies and gentlemen, with the ringing endorsement of Amelia Earhart to lift you, I wish you Godspeed in your good work toward greater heights.

PREFACE

DAVID HUMMELS

Many of us know the inequality numbers related to wages and women's representation on boards and at the highest levels of corporate hierarchies. It is a significant challenge, but it is also a tremendous educational opportunity. You just have to take a quick look at the relative trends in degree earners by gender and in women's labor-force participation to know that something has to give. Demographics can put enormous pressure on the workforce, and educational institutions and corporations need to engage in some rapid learning to make that adjustment possible.

This book draws on presentations and papers presented at the inaugural Leadership Excellence and Gender in Organizations Symposium that was held in the spring of 2016 at the Krannert School of Management at Purdue University, co-led with the Susan Bulkeley Butler Center for Leadership Excellence. It captures the first of what I hope will be an ongoing series of events bringing together leading academic thinkers with practitioners to examine leadership excellence and gender. I believe that a more dynamic two-way exchange between these camps will lead to more thoughtful and meaningfully directed scholarship, and to evidence-based improvements in corporate practice.

Moreover, I believe that Krannert and Purdue will continue to grow as a go-to location for that scholarship and for that exchange.

One of the reasons is that Purdue has a great history of graduating wildly successful alumnae, and in employing some tremendously talented women as academic leaders. Another reason is that it is now more important than ever for business and policymakers to focus on advancing gender and leadership. Professor Kossek and I were involved in a White House Summit a few years ago along with business deans from other top business schools and HR leaders. Krannert School of Management is committed to being a leader in this area and investing in events such as those that provided the content for this book. We believe inclusion is essential for any top-flight business school. Diversity helps bring different viewpoints to the classroom, deepening our students' understanding of today's business world.

CREATING GENDER-INCLUSIVE ORGANIZATIONS

INTRODUCTION: MAKING THE CASE FOR GENDER INCLUSION AND WOMEN'S CAREER EQUALITY AT WORK

ELLEN ERNST KOSSEK AND KYUNG-HEE LEE

Progress on gender diversity at work has stalled. To achieve equality, companies must turn good intentions into concrete action.

– Krivkovich et al., Women in the Workplace 2018 report

Although in recent years women have increased their occupational representation and upward mobility in the labor market, they remain under-leveraged as a source of talent and leadership in employing organizations in nearly every country around the globe. For example, women constitute only 4.6 percent of CEO positions and 19.2 percent of board directors at S&P (Standard and Poor) 500 companies (Catalyst, 2015). They hold only about one-fifth of the seats in Congress, including the Senate and House of Representatives (Center for American Woman and Politics, 2015). Despite their competence or experience, women are also under-utilized as a source of talent in many well-paid growing industries and jobs such as those in information technology (IT) where they occupy only 9 percent of senior IT roles (Graham, 2017).

The goal of this book is to add to the understanding of important issues involved in creating a gender-inclusive organization that helps support women's workplace advancement to leadership and significant professional roles. Its objectives are to bring together key thought leaders to bridge the research and practice knowledge gap on gender inclusion for students, researchers, managers, and organizations. It also seeks to advance understanding of how to build and sustain organizations that have a positive climate for gender inclusion that supports women's career equality.

Gender-Inclusive Organizational Climates

What is a gender-inclusive organizational climate? Gender-inclusive organizations with a positive climate for gender inclusion are those where members generally agree that leaders and organizational practices support and advance women's career equality (Kossek, Su, & Wu, 2017). Unfortunately, organizations greatly vary in the degree to which they make a strategic choice to actively support the gender inclusiveness of their climates. Kossek and colleagues (2017) at Purdue University reviewed hundreds of articles related to organizational gender inclusiveness. They developed a definition of a gender-inclusive climate based on several common themes prevalent in the management field. A gender-inclusive climate reflects "the degree to which individuals and organizational social groups perceive and experience the work environment as involving social interactions, cultures, and structures that are supportive of and effectively use the varied identities and values women bring to work, in ways that foster their belongingness and their abilities to leverage their talents to lead and contribute to the organization" (Kossek et al., 2017: 241).

Kossek and colleagues (2017) note that a gender-inclusive climate can lead to women's career equality, which has several dimensions. First, it is multilevel in that it involves individual, team, occupational, organizational, and societal processes. It can be measured at each of these levels, and dynamics at lower levels reflect higher-level nesting effects. For example, individual career experiences may be influenced by the dynamics of a woman's workgroup, team, occupation, organization, and society. When women are better represented across the firm and particularly at higher levels, individual women tend to have better career experiences as well (Joshi, Son, & Roh, 2015; Kanter, 1977).

Similarly, the concepts of gender inclusion such as ensuring fairness and non-discrimination, leveraging talent, and supporting women's values, interests, and needs (and voice) to foster belongingness involve individual, team, and organizational processes. For example, if women experience discrimination, it is likely that this is because a company's equal-opportunity policies related to selection, performance appraisal, or pay practices are not enforced, or not communicated or implemented well. Not only do individual, group, and organizational inclusion dynamics need to be better linked in practice and in action research, but initiatives must link concepts from different narratives on the enduring challenges holding women back from advancement. Three views are prevalent in the management literature: the discrimination view, which maintains that women often face gender bias challenges; the career preference view, which holds that many women have career orientations, interests, and values that differ from many men; and the work-family view, the perspective that women are held back because they still manage most of the domestic and family household responsibilities. These barriers are rarely linked in interventions designed to improve the three dimensions that are indicative of a gender-inclusive climate as depicted in figure 1.1 (Kossek et al., 2017).

The first dimension, *workplace fairness and equity for women*, reflects the degree to which organizations, managers, and employees generally agree that employment practices and policies are in place and leader actions are taken to foster equality and non-discrimination for women (Kossek & Zonia, 1993; Nishii, 2013: 242).

The second dimension, *leveraging women's talents to contribute and lead*, emerges from seminal research conducted by Ely and Thomas (2001). Their research suggests that inclusive organizations do not

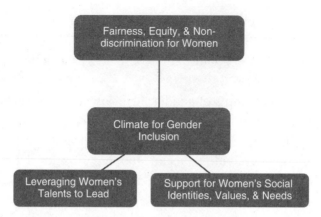

Figure 1.1. Characteristics of a Gender-Inclusive Climate

merely prevent bias to have women represented in managerial and professional roles or often hire women to mirror customers in the marketplace, but they create cultures of mutual learning and integration of women as part of the essence of firm culture. Gender-inclusive organizations go beyond this and develop strong norms where organizational members regularly learn from and incorporate women's knowledge, skills, and perspectives at work across all markets and business issues (Kossek et al., 2017). Women in such contexts experience high "person-environment fit" (Kristof-Brown & Billsberry, 2013). That is, women employees would generally see themselves as fitting in well with the values and roles of their jobs and the organization, and leaders and their peers would also hold these perceptions.

The third dimension relates to *having a workplace that women experience as socially supportive of women's identities, values, and needs.* These needs might include not only the support of work and family roles (Kossek, Pichler, Bodner, & Hammer, 2011) but also the support of psychological safety (Edmondson & Lei, 2014) for women to speak up, on issues that matter to them, without backlash or stigma. Women would collectively feel that they are empowered to be included in decision making at all levels of the organizational hierarchy (Nishii, 2013). Members would agree that there is high support for women's gender-related identities and that they would not have to sacrifice these identities (e.g., wife, mother, spouse) to be successful in the organization.

Women's Career-Equality Definition

Research suggests that highly gender-inclusive climates are a necessary condition for women to experience career equality. Women's career equality is defined as "the degree to which women, compared to men, (a) have equal access to and participation in career opportunities and (b) experience equal work and nonwork outcomes: both intrinsic (job, life, family satisfaction) and extrinsic (pay, promotions)" (Kossek et al., 2017: 229). For example, are women as likely as men to be considered and selected for leadership positions at all levels of the organization? Are they likely to get similar pay raises for similar performance? Compared to men, do women employees experience similarly positive job and family and life satisfaction and are they as likely to be married with children, if desired, and to have time to participate in meaningful non-work roles they care about? In order to achieve these goals, there needs to be greater integration of knowledge from scholars and practitioners regarding requisite actions for change.

Bridging Research to Practice

Unfortunately, research on gender inclusion often has not been effectively integrated into managerial and organizational practice. One reason for this persistent gap is that research on gender equality and inclusion often does a better job at *describing* problems in human resources practices, organizational structures, and climates than in coming up with evidence-based *solutions*. Similarly, for legal and social reasons, companies are probably reluctant to share their challenges and to allow widespread workplace access to scholars to help them determine how to improve women's under-utilization in the organization. For this book, we brought together thought leaders in academia and practice who have spent many years working on and/or researching issues related to gender and diversity in an effort to bridge this research-to-practice gap. The book grew out of an inaugural conference on women's career equality and leadership held at Purdue University and sponsored jointly by the Krannert School of Management and the Susan Bulkeley Butler Center for Leadership Excellence, and supported by many other campus sponsors, as well as a contribution from the Land of Lakes Corporation.

Organization of the Book

The book is organized into two main thematic parts, with an introduction at the beginning and an epilogue at the end. Part 1, "Fostering Positive Climates and Conversations," includes three chapters (chapters 2 to 4) that cover relational aspects of the organization. Chapter 2 examines research and practices on how to foster gender inclusion within and across national and global cultures. Chapter 3 addresses strategies for advancing women's careers and breaking glass ceilings, including quality mentoring and corporate initiatives to advance women. Chapter 4 focuses on how to build diverse teams and capitalize on the unexpected value of diversity.

Part 2, "Gender Inclusion in Industry and Organizational Contexts," turns our focus to specific contexts that we can learn from to understand specific environmental challenges related to gender inclusion. The first chapter in part 2 (chapter 5) examines issues in advancing women in general and women of color in the STEM (Science, Technology, Engineering, and Maths) fields. Chapter 6 addresses challenges in advancing women in very fast-paced environments, such as entrepreneurship and technology-based and other fast-growing industries.

Each chapter is organized as follows. The chapter starts with an essay from a leading researcher entitled "What the Research Tells Us." This is followed by a "View from Practice" essay by a senior human resources and diversity leader from a major leading global employer. The companies represented include Accenture, IBM, General Electric, PwC (formerly Price Waterhouse Coopers), and a major global internet commerce company. Next, an expert sums up key issues in an "Integrating Research and Practice" essay. Each chapter concludes with the editors' discussion of "Managerial and Organizational Actions" to create an inclusive environment by putting evidence-based research into practice. The book concludes with an epilogue (chapter 7) that discusses key themes of the book and provides an initial blueprint for organizations and researchers to advance gender inclusion, noting caveats related to fostering meaningful change.

Scope of the Book

This book is designed to open the conversation about how organizations and managers can take action to begin the journey to create a gender-inclusive organization, with the goal of supporting women's advancement to leadership. Our approach was to bring together experts who could bridge research and practice. In the book, we focused on the topics of gender-inclusive climates, mentoring, teamwork, and special areas such as STEM and entrepreneurial contexts. Of course, this book does not cover all the key issues related to gender inclusion. For example, the book has limited coverage of the lack of representation on top boards and the need for more examples of gender inclusion from outside North America and related to intersectionality. We plan to address these issues in later publications. As boundaries of this book, we focused on topics related to resources for gender inclusion and challenging contexts (STEM and entrepreneurship). We encourage readers to use the topics covered in this book as foundational knowledge. It is our hope that this book will be valuable to students, researchers, organizational leaders, and policymakers in jumpstarting change efforts to advance gender inclusion in the workplace.

REFERENCES

Catalyst. (2015). *Women CEOs of the S&P 500*. New York: Catalyst.

Center for American Women and Politics. (2015). http://www.cawp .rutgers.edu/women-us-congress-2015.

Edmondson, A., & Lei, Z. (2014). Psychological safety: The history, renaissance, and future of an interpersonal construct. *Annual Review of Organizational Psychology and Organizational Behavior, 1*, 23–43. https:// doi.org/10.1146/annurev-orgpsych-031413-091305

Ely, R.J., & Thomas, D.A. (2001). Cultural diversity at work: The effects of diversity perspectives on work group processes and outcomes. *Administrative Science Quarterly, 46*(2), 229–73. https://doi.org/10.2307 /2667087.

Graham, L. (2017, 22 May). Women take up just 9 percent of senior IT leadership roles, survey finds. Retrieved from https://www.cnbc .com/2017/05/22/women-take-up-just-9-percent-of-senior-it -leadership-roles-survey-finds.html.

Joshi, A., Son, J., & Roh, H. (2015). When can women close the gap? A meta-analytic test of sex differences in performance and rewards. *Academy of Management Journal, 58*(5), 1516–45. https://doi.org/10.5465 /amj.2013.0721.

Kanter, R.M. (1977). *Men and women of the corporation*. New York: Basic Books.

Kossek, E.E. (2016, 28 February). Organizer. Opening panel: Career agility: Making it work advice from the experts on career observations. Leadership Excellence and Gender in Organizations Conference,

Krannert School of Management and Susan Bulkeley Butler Center for Leadership Excellence at Purdue University. West Lafayette, IN.

Kossek, E.E., Pichler, S., Bodner, T., & Hammer, L.B. (2011). Workplace social support and work-family conflict: A meta-analysis clarifying the influence of general and work–family-specific supervisor and organizational support. *Personnel Psychology*, *64*(2), 289–313. https://doi.org/10.1111/j.1744-6570.2011.01211.x.

Kossek, E., Su, R., & Wu., L. (2017). "Opting out" or "pushed out"? Integrating perspectives on women's career equality for gender inclusion and interventions. *Journal of Management*, *43*(1), 228–54. https://doi.org/10.1177/0149206316671582.

Kossek, E.E., & Zonia, S.C. (1993). Assessing diversity climate: A field study of reactions to employer efforts to promote diversity. *Journal of Organizational Behavior*, *14*(1), 61–81. https://doi.org/10.1002/job.4030140107.

Kristof-Brown, A.L., & Billsberry, J. (2013). Fit for the future. In A. Kristof-Brown & J. Billsberry (Eds.), *Organizational fit: Key issues and new directions*, 1–18. Boston: Wiley.

Krivkovich, A., Nadeau, M., Robinson, K., Robinson, N., Strikeover, I., & Yee, L. (2018, October). Women in the workplace. Retrieved from https://www.mckinsey.com/featured-insights/gender-equality/women-in-the-workplace-2018.

Nishii, L.H. (2013). The benefits of climate for inclusion for gender diverse groups. *Academy of Management Journal*, *56*(6), 1754–74. https://doi.org/10.5465/amj.2009.0823.

PART ONE

Fostering Positive Climates and Conversations

2

CREATING GENDER-INCLUSIVE CLIMATES AND CONVERSATIONS

Diversity, or the state of being different, isn't the same as inclusion. One is a description of what is, while the other describes a style of interaction essential to effective teams and organizations.

– Bill Crawford, Leading Differently (Crawford, 2019)

What the Research Tells Us: The Role of Inclusive Climates in Closing the Gender Gap

LISA NISHII

Over the last decade, research and practice related to organizational diversity have expanded an emphasis on inclusion. This shift reflects the recognition that a mere focus on enhancing diverse representation by reducing "access discrimination" is insufficient; once hired, women and members of other historically marginalized groups often continue to experience various forms of "treatment discrimination" that constrain their engagement, ability, and motivation to contribute fully to their organizations, and ultimately limit their career outcomes. The ultimate goal of organizational efforts to enhance inclusion is to create integrative, multicultural work environments that not only limit experiences of treatment discrimination based on demographic background but also make it possible to leverage diversity's potential benefits. In inclusive climates, women and members of minority groups are treated as insiders with valued – rather than counter-normative – perspectives and strengths to contribute to the organization (Ely & Thomas, 2001; Davidson & Ferdman, 2001; Holvino, Ferdman, & Merrill-Sands, 2004; Nishii, 2013).

Despite widespread interest in inclusion, empirical research remains scarce, particularly with regard to the role of inclusive climates in closing the gender gap. The purpose of this chapter is to illustrate how inclusive climates impact outcomes for women at the individual and collective levels of analysis. With these lessons from research in mind, I will then discuss what I see to be the gaps between research and practice related to inclusion, and the implications for future research as well as practice.

Overview of Inclusive Climates

Research to date on inclusion falls into four broad categories: (1) organizational-level practices designed to promote employee inclusion (e.g., Roberson, 2006); (2) individual-level inclusion as defined by experiences of both belongingness and uniqueness (Shore et al., 2011); (3) the inclusiveness of workgroup climates (Nishii, 2013; Dwertmann, Nishii, & van Knippenberg, 2016); and (4) inclusive leadership, or the leadership behaviors that promote inclusive climates and experiences for employees (e.g., Nishii, Leroy, & Veestraten, 2014). As I discuss in more detail below, the focus of diversity and inclusion (D&I) work in organizations has, not surprisingly, been dominated by an identification of the practices and initiatives that are thought to promote better inclusion for employees, with less careful attention being paid to assessing employee experiences of inclusion, inclusive leadership behaviors, and the inclusiveness of workgroup climates (Nishii, Khattab, Shemla, & Paluch, 2018). Perhaps a related challenge is that the representation of women and minorities in senior leadership is often viewed by organizations as evidence of inclusion, a perception that serves to blur the conceptual distinction between diversity and inclusion. This distinction is non-trivial: whereas diversity relates to equal-opportunity goals associated with the hiring, advancement, and retention of individuals representing diverse social identity groups, inclusion is a relational construct derived from experiences of social belonging and being valued for one's uniqueness (Shore et al., 2011). Although inclusion in senior leadership is certainly one of the hoped-for outcomes of inclusion, it is not in and of itself evidence of inclusion, as it is possible for women and minorities to advance or be hired into senior positions in spite of low levels of inclusion within the organizational context, and also because once in senior leadership positions, it is possible for women and minorities to lack experiences of social, informational, and psychological inclusion that are commensurate with those of their male peers.

This disconnect represents the greatest opportunity for organizations for at least two reasons. First, there is little evidence that the implementation of D&I practices alone can guarantee experiences of inclusion, or even significant improvements in representation in senior leadership (Kalev, Dobbin, & Kelly, 2006; Nishii et al., 2018). Second, within a single organization with the same D&I practices, the inclusiveness of workgroup climates can vary widely, with differences in climate being what account for people's experiences of inclusion. As the well-known Gallup studies show, people tend to leave their organizations primarily because of poor experiences with their supervisor and/or co-workers (Harter, Schmidt, & Keyes, 2003), experiences that are more proximally influenced by climate than by organizational practices. This is echoed by research on engagement which shows that the psychological meaningfulness of one's work and the psychological safety and availability one experiences at work (both of which, again, are intimately related to workgroup climate) are more important drivers of engagement than elements of the broader employment contract as defined by organizational practices (Kahn, 1990; Macey & Schneider, 2008; Macey,

Schneider, Barbera, & Young, 2009). Together, this evidence suggests that organizations that adopt a multipronged approach to inclusion that involves not just the implementation of D&I best practices but also careful attention to developing inclusive climates and leaders are most likely to succeed in enhancing the inclusion and advancement of women.

As a means of illustrating the potential gains for organizations in focusing (additional) efforts on developing and maintaining inclusive workgroup climates, I briefly review some of my research on inclusive climates. My conceptualization and measurement of inclusive climates in this research consist of three dimensions: (1) *Fairly implemented employment practices* that signify a level playing field rather than perpetuate demographically based status differentials within organizations (Greenhaus et al., 1990); (2) *Integration of differences,* or the openness with which employees enact and engage their "whole" selves without fear of consequences (Ragins, 2008) and without having to conform to the dominant group in order to be accepted (Shore et al., 2011); and (3) *Inclusion in decision making,* or the extent to which the diverse perspectives of employees are actively sought and incorporated in an effort to facilitate collective learning (Ely & Thomas, 2001).

The focus of inclusive climates differs from more traditional notions of diversity climate in a couple of key ways. First, most existing operationalizations of diversity climate focus on the existence of equal employment opportunity practices, fair treatment, and the absence of discrimination in the employment process. While the first dimension of climate for inclusion also focuses on fairness, it departs from most other assessments of diversity climate in its attention to the nature of interpersonal exchanges and group process norms that are essential for promoting positive, synergistic outcomes associated with diversity (Dwertmann et al., 2016). Second, while most research on diversity climate has involved individuals' assessments of organizational-level D&I initiatives (i.e., fair implementation of HR practices, diversity-specific programs aimed at improving employment outcomes for members of marginalized groups, visible efforts on the part of senior leaders to reduce discrimination), climate for inclusion captures individuals' perceptions of their more proximal work-group context. The underlying logic is that inclusion is not just about whether individuals feel fairly treated or accepted within their organization. People's everyday experiences of inclusion at work are largely determined by the extent to which unit-level motivations, norms, and accountability structures make it likely that employees will engage in personalized as opposed to stereotype-based interactions with their co-workers, and in so doing, open up the possibility of learning from diverse others to leverage the synergistic potential offered by their diversity (Page, 2007).

Implications of Inclusive Climates for Individual and Group Outcomes

Decades of research have demonstrated the persistence of gender biases in organizations, with men enjoying better treatment, greater access to resources and opportunities, inclusion in networks of influence, better fit, and overall higher levels of employment success than women (Cox, 1993). These findings are most commonly explained by psychological theories of social identity and social categorization (Tajfel & Turner, 1986; Williams & O'Reilly, 1998) according to which it is assumed that categorizations of others based on demographic attributes result almost automatically in biases that favor higher-status "in-group" members over outgroup members. In-group members tend to command more respect, deference, and power than outgroup members, and to experience greater fit with the norms and practices of the dominant organizational culture (Bargh & Chartrand, 1999). Consequently, they are also more likely to receive the benefit of the doubt when it comes to evaluations of competence and leadership potential. As members of the lower-status outgroup, women and members of minority groups often feel pressure to adopt facades of conformity (Hewlin, 2003; 2009) in order to try to be accepted, have a harder time experiencing fit and inclusion, and are at risk of being assumed to be less competent than their male peers (Heilman, 2001). Further, because in-group-outgroup distinctions can breed negative affect and competition (Brewer, 1999), women are also more at risk of experiencing discrimination and/or more subtle forms of social undermining from co-workers (Duffy, Ganster, & Pagon, 2002). Research also suggests that because men (and whites) are more likely to be demographically similar to their managers, they are also more likely to be included in the manager's in-group (e.g., Tsui & O'Reilly, 1989), as seen in the development of higher-quality leader-subordinate relationships (Gerstner & Day, 1997). Even if men are not demographically similar to their managers, the stereotype-based expectation that men are more competent than women makes them more attractive for managerial investments of resources (Eden, 1992; Heilman, 2001).

These theories and related empirical findings paint a rather grim picture when it comes to closing the gender gap. Luckily, theory from sociology offers insight about the conditions under which the aforementioned gender biases are less likely. According to status characteristics theory (Ridgeway, 1991; Ridgeway & Correll, 2006), identity differences among group members are psychologically meaningful only when they are correlated with status rankings and access to resources in ways that reinforce historical and societal trends (e.g., women and ethnic minorities having less authority: DiTomaso et al., 2007; Ridgeway, 1991). Thus, to the extent that the inclusiveness of a unit's climate delegitimizes socio-historical status hierarchies within the unit context, identity characteristics like gender can lose their psychological significance so that they no longer trigger the social categorization processes that result in stereotyping and biased treatment. In addition, because of the value that is placed on self-expression as a means of engaging in deep learning (Ely & Thomas, 2001), employees in inclusive climates feel psychologically safe enough to be authentic. By sharing their personal identities, they are more likely to foster interpersonal trust (Ensari & Miller, 2006) and experience self-verification (Polzer, Milton, & Swann, 2002). As a result, feelings of inclusion should increase, and incidents of incivility should disappear. Furthermore, in an inclusive climate in which employees and managers share a commitment to utilizing people's unique identities as a source of insight and learning, managers should be more likely to establish high-quality relationships with all employees, despite demographic backgrounds (Nishii & Mayer, 2009).

Consistent with this, across a variety of public and private organizations, I have found that overall, male (as well as white) employees tend to report experiencing significantly higher-quality relationships with their supervisors, perceived fit of their values and abilities with their job, self-verification (or feeling that co-workers perceive them in ways that are consistent with the way they see themselves), and perceived organizational support, in addition to lower levels of discrimination and incivility. However, study results also show that these gender- and race-based differences largely disappear within the context of inclusive workgroup climates and, therefore, so do associated differences in organizational commitment and turnover (e.g., Nishii, 2011). What this suggests is that in inclusive climates, women (and ethnic minorities) are less likely to be treated as outsiders and seen as representatives of overly simplistic stereotypes; they find it easier to identify personally with their workgroup's identity because they are more fully integrated into the shaping of it.

Interestingly, it is not just female employees who benefit from working in inclusive climates. Because inclusive climates help to neutralize demographically based disparities and the salience of associated subgroups, units with inclusive climates tend to experience higher overall levels of group cohesion, and therefore higher productivity (Gully, Devine, & Whitney, 1995; Summers, Coffelt, & Horton, 1988). Furthermore, because group members feel psychologically safe enough to be authentic and experience interpersonal trust, they tend to be more open to different perspectives and engage in constructive, task-related debate (van Knippenberg, de Dreu, & Homan, 2004). In data collected from thousands of workgroups from multiple diverse samples – including a global hotel chain, three federal agencies, and a large plumbing wholesaler – I have consistently found that workgroups with inclusive climates indeed report higher levels of cohesion and engage in more information elaboration (Nishii & Bruyere, 2013; Nishii & Langevin, 2009; Nishii, Leroy, & Simons, 2014; Nishii, McAlpine, Rubineau, & Bruyere, 2015). In the case of the plumbing wholesaler, where branch-level sales data were available, information elaboration and group cohesion were in turn associated with improved financial performance. In contrast, the negative social categorization effects that are perpetuated by status inequalities are manifested in the form of treatment disparities and social disintegration in units that lack inclusive climates. Within such units, employees tend to be unable or unwilling to share information in ways that enhance performance, to the detriment of both majority and minority employees.

In an effort to better understand how the inclusiveness of workgroup climates impacts individual and group outcomes through its influence on the nature of interpersonal interactions and relationships, in a follow-up study, I utilized a social-networks approach (Nishii et al., 2015). I expected that in workgroups that lack inclusive climates, the pattern of social ties within a workgroup would be illustrative of social categorization effects. In other words, individuals would be more likely to report demographically similar others as close friends and key resources, such that subgroups based on demographic identities would be evident in the data. In inclusive climates, however, I expected that people would develop more cross-boundary relationships. In support of these expectations, I found that in inclusive climates, people develop a significantly higher proportion of social network ties with demographically dissimilar co-workers. Here, the reference point was the total possible demographically dissimilar ties an individual could conceivably develop within his/her workgroup based on the level of diversity in gender, race, and disability status present in the workgroup. The more important contribution of this study, however, was in showing that not only do individuals in inclusive climates develop more ties with dissimilar co-workers, but those ties with dissimilar co-workers are also of significantly better quality than is the case in units that lack inclusive climates. More specifically, workers are more likely to report that they feel well understood personally, experience high levels of mutual trust, and feel that it is psychologically safe to disagree with the other person. That inclusive climates nurture the development of personalized, high-trust relationships with dissimilar others is critical for the advancement of women and minorities because it is the traditional lack of such personalized relationships across in-group-outgroup boundaries that fuels the perpetuation of stereotypes that disadvantage women and limit their contributions (Nishii, 2015; Nishii et al., 2015). Indeed, the data showed that women who were freed from traditional in-group-outgroup boundaries (as evidenced by their high-quality dissimilar relationships) were more committed and engaged than women who were not, and also benefited from higher levels of group cohesion and information elaboration within their workgroups.

When women and minorities are no longer seen as mere representatives of their social identity group, negative stereotypes about competence are less likely to be imposed on them; that is, it is more likely that others will be able to recognize and value their unique strengths and abilities (Ensari & Miller, 2005, 2006; Kanter, 1977). As such, they should also be less prone to the disadvantaging effects of negative self-prophecies and should receive more credit for their contributions and successes (Eden, 1993; Heilman, Block, & Lucas, 1992; Heilman, 2001). It can be challenging to test this empirically, however, as individual performance ratings are usually fiercely guarded by organizations. In one study with a high-tech materials manufacturing firm, however, I was able to link survey responses with performance ratings provided by the organization and found that not only do women and minorities report significantly more favorable work attitudes (e.g., fit, inclusion, perceived organizational support, commitment, engagement) in inclusive climates, they also receive higher performance ratings than peers working in less inclusive climates. These results suggest that high levels of performance that may otherwise be overly scrutinized, discounted, or trigger a likability penalty in traditional contexts because of their counter-stereotypical nature may more readily be recognized and rewarded in inclusive climates.

More in-depth analyses aimed at identifying the most significant barriers to the advancement of women into senior leadership positions within this same firm provided further evidence of how inclusive organizational climates and inclusive leadership behaviors that help to promote them may positively impact the career advancement of women and minorities. Given research that has shown that challenging developmental experiences are critical for advancement into senior positions (DeRue & Wellman, 2009; Dragoni, Tesluk, Russell, & Oh, 2009), a primary goal of the research was to examine whether low levels of female representation in senior leadership could be explained by gender differences in access to key challenging developmental experiences. The underlying logic was that because stretch assignments by definition involve greater risk and require more resilience than typical assignments, they may evoke more male-type attributes than would otherwise be the case, thereby exacerbating the negative outcomes of "role incongruence" for women (e.g., Eagly & Karau, 2002; Ragins & Sundstrom, 1989).

Initial analyses revealed that those individuals who had successfully advanced to the top three layers of management could be distinguished from those who hadn't by their exposure to five challenging developmental experiences – such as having to make high-stakes decisions, needing to exert influence on people over whom one has little formal authority, and inheriting problems from a predecessor – at key points within their careers. Follow-up analyses designed to evaluate whether gender predicts the probability of being assigned to these key developmental experiences (after controlling for job function) revealed that indeed it does. Gender differences emerge starting at around age thirty when men are between 25 and 50 percent more likely to report having challenging developmental experiences. Over the next two decades, disparities snowball until the differential increases to as high as 165 percent for high-risk and high-stakes assignments. Interestingly, however, gender differences were attenuated in parts of the organization with more inclusive aggregate climates.

Combined with results from separate but related analyses which revealed that employees who work in inclusive climates have stronger leadership aspirations, these data tell an important story about how experiences of inclusion impact advancement. In inclusive climates, women are more likely to experience self-verification and develop authentic relationships in which they feel that their unique qualities are recognized and valued, including relationships with dissimilar co-workers and with their supervisors. These high-quality relationships help fuel work-related efficacy and engagement, both of which are critical drivers of performance. Better-quality relationships and performance define a cycle of success in which individuals are deemed worthy of performance feedback and mentoring and become noticed as having leadership potential. As Ibarra and colleagues (2013) have argued, being seen by others as a potential leader is critical for transforming one's identity from that of an individual contributor to an actual leader – something that is an essential condition for advancing successfully into senior leadership.

Conclusions

Altogether, this body of research suggests that to the extent that the commonly adopted set of diversity management practices is more aligned with diversity than with inclusion goals (Nishii et al.,

2018), more of the same is unlikely to have as great an impact on closing the gender gap as the adoption of an expanded set of practices targeted specifically at shaping inclusive climates. As Bromley and Powell (2012) explain, when policies are ineffective at driving hoped-for outcomes, there are two possible explanations. One is policy-practice decoupling, and the other is means-end decoupling. Whereas the former assumes that policies and practices are appropriately designed for achieving the outcomes of interest but fail to achieve intended goals due to the suboptimal implementation of those policies, the latter highlights the possibility that policies may be ineffective because they are decoupled from what is needed to achieve the strategic goals of interest. In other words, because the *right* set of practices is not in place. This is not to say that traditional diversity management or equal-opportunity practices – such as targeted recruiting, diversity training, mentoring, and work-life benefits – are not important or needed, because they are. However, they are likely necessary but insufficient for closing the gender gap through the inclusion-related pathways described above because they are not adequately focused on transforming the socio-relational context in ways that are essential for reducing stereotyping and prejudice (Green & Kalev, 2008; Nishii, 2013).

View from Practice: The Power of "Staying versus Leaving" Conversations to Create an Inclusive Work Environment at Accenture

NELLIE BORRERO

I was born and raised in New York City in the Bronx, one of the boroughs of New York City, and I was the first one to go to college in my family. I was the first one to join the corporate environment. So it was quite interesting. My first day of work, I had no one to really help me prepare for this new corporate environment that I was about to enter. The company that I was at was Arthur Andersen, now known as Accenture, and I remember getting on the train and going into the city from the Bronx in 1986. On my first day, I walked into the orientation room where everybody was sitting. There were about forty people in the room. The company environment was very conservative at the time. All of the men were wearing navy blue suits with their ties and their white shirt. All the women in the office were also wearing their navy suits with a white shirt and their pearls. I walked in with a satin tangerine suit. The suit had six large bow buttons, and I was wearing earrings that would hit my cheek when I turned my head. My shoes were black, orange, and yellow. That was how I walked into my first corporate job. I was pulled aside by my supervisor at the time, and he said, "Nellie, welcome," and I said, "Thank you," and he said, "You look like the curtains in my living room," and I said, "Those must be some nice curtains." Soon after this interaction, I immediately felt like something was off, and that feeling just kept going for a few months. I felt as if I did not belong. Three months after I started working at the company, I told my supervisor that it was just not working for me. He asked me why, and I told him that I just did not fit in. I had an accent, and people just did not understand what I was saying. My supervisor responded to my decision to leave by saying, "Nellie, you may either leave and potentially face this challenge someplace else, or you can stay and help change the culture here." Fast-forward to today, and it has been almost thirty years since I started at Accenture. I look back and remember how I started, which was a place of not belonging, a place of a lot of fear, and a place of a lot of not feeling confident every day. For me, diversity is very personal. At Accenture, we highly value inclusion and diversity. We want to promote an environment where everyone that enters our doors feels that they have an opportunity to reach their goals no matter what difference they represent, and for us, that is critically important. It is all about inclusion, and it is about ensuring that we have the diversity to work with that inclusion.

The journey of diversity is what I would like to focus on in this essay. The journey for me has had five stages, and the stages are as follows. First, when diversity became the buzzword in the late eighties and early nineties in the United States and the United Kingdom, it started out as *a nice thing to do*. People viewed it as a fad that would go away within a year or two. However, it did not go away. From this, diversity then became *the right thing to do*, the second stage. Companies tried to go beyond being nice and do the right thing, and focus on diversity. Following this stage, the question became what *the business case* was. In this third stage, there were more discussions around the return on investment and the value of diversity. The business case was clear. It was about hiring, attracting, and retaining the best people. We got past the business case stage. Following these stages, the fourth stage was about finding *who was accountable* for inclusion and diversity. We had interesting conversations with many people within our organization, engaging our legal, marketing, and human resources groups, and reached the discussion of "do not tell me how we cannot do this and tell me how we can."

So today, we are in a different stage. We have passed the stages of being nice, doing right, developing the business case, and finding accountability. Today the message is that inclusion and diversity are *everyone's responsibility*. It does not matter where you sit in whatever part of the organization, what you think you have or do not have, or what part of the world you sit in. Everyone is responsible for creating an inclusive environment.

There is still work to be done. For example, people tend to call programs related to diversity "special programs" whether it is a women's program or a program focusing on ethnic minorities. When we hear people talk about special programs for people who have diverse backgrounds, no matter what segment that is, we need to challenge that because it is not about something special. Inclusion and diversity are a business imperative that we are all responsible to fix. At Accenture, we are aligning strategies and programs that are going to help us close those gaps. You have to have the courage to advocate for people on a daily basis, and I would say if you don't have the courage to challenge leaders, peers, and the culture that you're in, then you're in the wrong part of the business because you have to be courageous.

Within Accenture, there are now 180,000 women globally. There are programs that are focused on women across various cultures and backgrounds. Working at Accenture, I have worked all over the world, visiting places that I would have never thought about, and what that has taught me is that for women, no matter where they are sitting, in whatever part of the world, in whatever culture, the commonality is that we want to continue to aspire and reach our goals because we want to be able to contribute to our family. If we have children, we want to be able to provide for our children. In some cultures, it is not just your own children. It is your nieces and nephews. It is about giving. It is about empowering. In order to do that, we have to have transparent conversations. These conversations have to be centered on the things that are negatively impacting women, things that must be changed. The challenges are the various cultural norms. There are things that you are expected to do. There are things you are expected not to do. Organizations need to impact without changing that culture. It is a balance that we have to work through because we want to make sure we are respectful of people's cultures, but we want to make sure that we're also motivating people to aspire for more. Through programs and through conversations, we can achieve this and reach the goal and impact equality, whether it is for people within Accenture or people within the community. We can create more opportunities for young girls around the world, but also for boys. It is about everyone.

Any organization experiences attrition. When we have conversations with women about their decision to leave, we hear different stories depending on what part of the world we are in. In some cases, it is as simple as women deciding that they want to do something different. In other cases, these women decide that this is just way too hard. It also could be the push-pull factors, where women are being pulled from their responsibilities at home, and they are getting the push within the organization because they are not being aligned to the right roles. In the push-pull situations, we have focused on what we call "stay conversations" within our organization around the world. Just as I did thirty years ago, many women still go into the office of their leader and say, "I'm resigning," but they lack the confidence to go into the office of their leader and say, "How can you help me stay? Here are the things that I need to be able to stay. Here's what I need to be able to have this work-life integration." I believe in work-life integration rather than work-life balance because it is about how you integrate it and what you decide to do on any given day or in any given week, month, and year. Leaders have the power through their words and actions to change and turn the "leave conversation" into a "stay conversation," as my supervisor did thirty years ago for me.

At Accenture, we have had these conversations with women, and what we discovered is that the needs are very different in different parts of the world. The "stay conversations" in India can be different than in other parts of the world. There are responsibilities that young women have once they get into the situation of marriage that other cultures may not experience. Companies have to be able to adjust to these differences within cultures. In South Africa, the challenges and ways to empower women are different than those in India. There are challenges in some parts of the world that are issues of safety. So how can we empower women to have that safety? What do we put into play for that safety? These are the kinds of conversations that must be had in order to understand and make a change. Regardless of what country or culture we are talking about, leaders at the top have to believe in this change and conversation. They have to be able to lead it with courage, and they have to advocate.

To improve inclusion and diversity, it is important for an organization to have clearly stated aspirations, goals, and objectives. They could be centered on women, or they could be centered on ethnic minorities. At Accenture, we have aspirational objectives with our Lesbian/Gay/Bisexual/Transgender community, military, and persons with disabilities. At Accenture, we get into conversations that help us create a transforming environment. These conversations are never punitive. We approach these conversations as dialogue because we have to showcase how we are faring within our own businesses, and that has been very helpful.

Having a mass of women leaders at the top has been very effective for fostering change. When you start to get the representation that represents the difference in masses, it makes a significant change. During the past fiscal year, we promoted many women into high-level roles within Accenture. Among these women at the top, there was a new discussion around our maternity policy. As a company, we wanted to continue to create an environment where women feel empowered, but we also wanted to inform men about paternity leave as well. In discussion, we realized that, in the United States, policy is really short for women and non-existent for men. In order to make changes, we looked at the numbers and made the decision to go beyond the government mandate and provide four months of paid maternity leave for women in the United States. From there, we looked at our offices around the world and began changing the policy in India, Argentina, and the Philippines and are now looking at more countries. It is important that, as a company, we do not assume that every woman *wants* to be out for four months, but now we can *offer* them the ability to be out for four months. We also do not want to assume that when women come back, they do not want to travel or they do want to travel. We took a step further. At Accenture, for women who come back after their four months' paid leave, if they do not want to travel, we guarantee them a local assignment, so they do not have to travel. If they want to travel while they are breastfeeding, we pay for the shipment of their breast milk. When there is representation at the top – leaders who have influence, who can make the change – then you start to see the culture changes. No matter where you are going to sit in whatever part of an organization or educational institution or whatever your career of choice is, you have the power to have the conversation to help change the environment you operate in, if not for yourself, for those who are going to follow. There is power in numbers, and there is power in people having conversations.

When it comes to leadership and how leaders look at different cultures, it is critically important for us to recognize that we are not always going to get it right. We are not perfect. We are human. Many leaders do not want to have a conversation to get to the issue at hand because they are afraid of offending someone. They do not want to say the wrong thing, and they do not want to be misinterpreted. To avoid this, at Accenture, we have many different levels of awareness, and we focus on one in particular for all our leaders globally: leading a diverse workforce. Wherever you are, you will lead a diverse workforce. At Accenture, we are focused on how to equip our leaders globally to lead a diverse workforce. We talk about the unconscious biases that we have. It is important to understand that we all have an unconscious bias. At Accenture, we address this issue by talking about micro-inequity. Leaders with so many multiple competing priorities may not take the time to really understand how they may be offending someone or how they may be excluding someone. At Accenture, those conversations about micro-inequity have been very transparent. Leaders come in and ask questions about why diversity is important or how to talk about sensitive issues such as LGBT or disabilities. I believe that it is important to continue to have this dialogue because that is the only way we are going to be able to learn and empower inclusion within our workforce.

In conclusion, we need to remember that no matter where you are going to sit in whatever part of an organization, you have the power to have the conversation to help change the environment you operate in, if not for yourself, for those who are going to follow. There is power in numbers and there is power in people having important conversations.

Integrating Research and Practice: Gender-Inclusive Climates

CHARLICE HURST

Conversations about advancing women's leadership tend to treat the experience of being a woman as uniform across cultures, ethnicities, and other categories of difference. Certainly, there are numerous commonalities among women worldwide. Across societies, the structure of gender relations has resulted in a paucity of women in leadership across most major institutions. However, the specific cultural norms, values, and economic conditions under which women live vary considerably. Therefore, initiatives that work well in the United States may need to be tweaked – or even overhauled – to achieve success in other countries. Dr Lisa Nishii's essay provided extensive and compelling findings regarding the role of inclusive climates in creating conditions for women's ascent to leadership positions, and Nellie Borrero, managing director of Global Inclusion and Diversity at Accenture, illustrates a climate for inclusion in practice in multinational organizations. However, as the statistics on women's presence in leadership in most countries reveal, most companies are not engaging in these practices. Even companies that are being proactive continue to experience gaps, just as Borrero described. Women are still having a "leave conversation" rather than a "stay conversation," as Borrero did thirty years ago. What further light can researchers shed on tactics for accelerating progress, particularly in non-U.S. settings?

It seems worthwhile for organizations to consider where they stand relative to the dimensions of Nishii's model of inclusive climates (Nishii, 2013), adapting it to local contexts. For instance, organizations would need to review what constitutes fair employment practices in a particular country. This could require exceeding conformance with human resources laws, as such laws may not sufficiently address issues related to gender equity. With regard to integrating diverse identities, consideration must be given to what identities employees are bringing to work. Obviously, countries differ in their demographic makeup. They also differ in standards for disclosing identities. For instance, people raised in the United States tend to self-disclose more rapidly than Japanese people (Schug, Yuki, & Maddux, 2010). This might affect the extent to which employees perceive it as appropriate for the organization to invite personal sharing. Although achieving a distinct identity is important in most cultures, people in individualistic cultures like the United States tend to establish their uniqueness on the basis of differences in personal characteristics, while people in collectivistic cultures do so by emphasizing their social position (Becker et al., 2012).

A collectivistic culture may conflict with the need to disassociate gender from status differences. In most cultures, women are subordinates across institutional contexts, from the home to the workplace. When employees prioritize social position in their relationships at work, they might tend to maintain this hierarchy. For instance, one often hears of the phenomenon of female employees taking responsibility for tasks at work that are domestic in nature, such as organizing social gatherings and bringing in food to share. This may reduce time spent on tasks that are more highly rewarded by the organization and may also position women as subordinate within their workgroups. However, expecting people who are collectivistic to relate based on personal qualities may undermine their preferences for establishing and communicating their identity. Thus, doing so is inconsistent with the idea that a climate for inclusion supports people in defining themselves in the way that they choose. When such a conflict exists between enabling authentic

identity expression and preventing the reproduction of gender inequalities, it might be even more important for organizations to ensure that their practices are fair. Moreover, they might benefit from
sending a message that authentic identity expression is valued but
also from challenging employees to question and disrupt workplace
behaviors that undermine the company's clear commitment to gender equity.

Inclusion in decision making, the final dimension in Nishii's
(2013) model, may be affected by cultural differences in power distance, which refers to expectations regarding the hierarchical distribution of authority (Hofstede, Hofstede, & Minkov, 1991). High
power-distance cultures are characterized by greater acceptance of
inequities in power. People from such cultures may be uncomfortable with decision-making processes that reduce distinctions in authority between employees and managers (Farh, Hackett, & Liang,
2007). There is evidence that reducing status differences between
managers and employees can backfire, reducing the performance
and altruism of subordinates high in power distance (Farh et al.,
2007). Thus, in high power-distance cultures, employers may need
to reconsider how to benefit from the perspectives of employees
without violating expectations regarding the proper roles of leader
and follower.

Although Nishii's (2013) model seems to be a promising starting
point for organizations seeking to advance women, it is important
to proceed with caution. As Ayman and Korabik (2010) point out,
simply imposing leadership theories developed in the context of the
United States on very different cultures may fail to capture nuances
and may marginalize local perspectives. To counter this, organizations might establish mechanisms to listen very closely to local reactions to their initiatives and adjust nimbly. The careful explanation
behind the reason for inclusion initiatives is also key, as Accenture
has found. Observing Accenture's diversity and inclusion approach,
it seems that practice has moved ahead of research, perhaps because

of the urgency of aligning culture with strategy in diverse settings and the limitations researchers face in obtaining data and publishing relevant research. Pointing to the limitations of cross-sectional research, Nishii called for organizations to welcome researchers to conduct randomized controlled studies and described one in which she and a colleague are training team leaders in cultivating inclusive climates and using a mobile app for the training and assessment of teams over a five-month period. Yet there is still much to learn from existing research, and the potential learning is certainly not covered exhaustively here. Nevertheless, the necessity of accelerating women's advancement into leadership positions demands that organizations apply the best available evidence, while seeking to continue generating knowledge.

Managerial and Organizational Actions for Creating Inclusive Climates

ELLEN ERNST KOSSEK AND KYUNG-HEE LEE

Managerial Actions

• **Engage in and model inclusive employee conversations.**
Managers play a crucial role in creating an inclusive climate. It starts with managers' learning how to develop conversations that are inclusive of subordinates of diverse backgrounds across their entire team, where individuals feel that they have the psychological safety to engage in authentic conversations – the ability to share what they truly think and feel.

Conversations involve at least two people. Even when managers try to have inclusive conversations, employees may not be willing to open up to them. A recent study involving interviews with more than 300 employees by Phillips, Dumas, and Rothbard (2018) found that minority employees often do not feel comfortable sharing their personal information with colleagues or their supervisors. The study found that one of the reasons why minority employees are hesitant to share their personal information is that they fear sharing personal information will emphasize their differences, resulting in isolating them rather than helping them belong to the group. This is an important barrier to creating an inclusive work climate, because inclusive culture means employees feel they belong while simultaneously feeling appreciated for their uniqueness (Shore et al., 2011).

Phillips and colleagues (2018) suggest several tips for managers to help foster inclusive conversations. The first tip is starting formal and informal gatherings with ice-breaker activities to reduce stress as people interact with others whom they don't know well, while helping them get to know each other. Formal ice-breaker activities can help individuals feel comfortable navigating social events, especially those where they are in the minority. There are many team-building activities available (cf Heathfield, 2019), but try to start out with ice-breakers that aren't too intrusive yet foster safe self-disclosure to support working together. An example might be having people interview a partner to find at least one common interest they share and one that is different.

A second tip is to *take a learning approach* – defined as engaging in conversations with genuine curiosity and openness without preconceived notions, particularly when talking with employees with a different background than one's own. For example, if a male manager is chatting about last night's football game with some male employees in the break room when a female employee enters, rather than assuming that she is uninterested and continuing the conversation with only the male employees, some managers might try to be inclusive by asking the female employee whether she likes football. While this is well-intended, it could backfire and exclude her from the conversation if she says "no"; so an even more open approach might be asking her what kind of sports she likes to play or watch.

This latter question conveys that the manager genuinely wants to engage in conversation without any preconceived notions.

- **When managing subordinates' performance, take actions to prevent unconscious biases, increase decision-making transparency, and foster career-opportunity equity.**

Research shows that employees' beliefs that they have a positive relationship with and are fairly treated by their manager increase their perceptions of an inclusive work climate over time (Brimhall, Mor Barak, Hurlburt, McArdle, Palinkas, & Henwood, 2017). Yet ensuring these perceptions may be challenging, as managers are increasingly likely to manage employees who differ from them in gender and in cultural or other backgrounds. These salient social identity differences may play into subordinates' perceptions (and realities) of unfairness – namely, that managers are sometimes seen to unconsciously favor some employees and give them better assignments or promotions. In fact, this differential treatment can be based on managers' own assessment of each employee's merits, which, in turn, may indeed be based on implicit bias. The evidence bears out that women and other underrepresented employees tend to receive less favorable assessments and fewer developmentally challenging assignments (see Nishii, in this chapter). When employees perceive that their work assignments are not fairly allocated and do not see a clear rationale for the differential treatment, it is very difficult to create an inclusive culture (Ford & Seers, 2006).

One tactic that managers can use in order to combat the problem is to have transparent conversations regarding the criteria upon which differential decisions about career opportunities are based. Other strategies include identifying and facilitating developmental opportunities to enable women and employees from minority groups to gain the requisite background, or enabling individuals to demonstrate competencies by substituting other life experiences. A recent study (Chen, He, & Weng, 2018) found that when employees understand clearly why certain employees get favorable work assignments or promotions based on their productivity, skills, or work ethic, they have more buy-in and support for the differential treatment. Such conversations can also lead to additional dialogue on how to work together to increase developmental opportunities and skills.

Increasing inclusive dialogue with your employees helps foster transparency and accountability in employee evaluation and promotion decisions. Before you make your work assignment and promotion decisions, think about how you would explain your work assignment and promotion decisions to others. By doing this exercise, you may realize that you unconsciously have been favoring certain groups of people over others. In closing, managers need to remember that a *conversation is a powerful tool for creating an inclusive work climate, whether it is personal friendly small talk or a conversation about how to address diversity-climate problems.* Open and transparent conversations are the basis of a trusting working relationship between a manager and employees that leads to an inclusive working climate. Remember that managers play a key role in creating an inclusive and supportive work climate (Kossek, Pichler, Bodner, & Hammer, 2011) and have the power to change diverse employees' "leave conversations" to "stay conversations."

Organizational Actions

- **Educate leaders and members to increase the ability to identify and address diversity and inclusion policy and practice "decoupling" gaps.**
A difficulty many organizations face as they try to enhance diversity and inclusion is that the organization may experience what we refer to as "decoupling" or "disconnects" between formal and informal organizational practices and processes. Having these gaps can foster employee cynicism and tensions in creating a positive climate for diversity, and may hinder effectiveness.

Decoupling gaps affecting the climate can occur in three forms: (a) between formal policy and diverse employees' perceived inclusion needs; (b) between structural demographic change to increase workforce diversity and the prevailing leader and group cultural values, biases, and practices; and (c) between posted policies and actual implementation. We elaborate on each of these gaps below.

- **Conduct an audit to identify gaps between formal diversity and inclusion policies and experiences of relevant employee groups, and communicate HR policies clearly to increase transparency.**

First, companies need to assess the extent of decoupling between formal diversity and inclusion policies and employees' inclusion needs and experiences of climate. Well-intentioned diversity policies may not produce desired outcomes because the organization focused more on hiring diverse applicants than on ensuring that measures to address implicit bias and ensure transparency of HR policies were increased to support inclusion. A common example of a diversity policy not aligning well with diverse employees' needs is the early diversity recruitment policy efforts that some firms followed in the 1990s (and that many still follow today) that emphasize hiring more women and people from other underrepresented groups to meet hiring targets, without concomitantly taking steps to make the diverse employees feel valued and that they have access to resources they need to advance in the organization. Companies that only hire diverse workers without linking recruitment policies to HR policies such as performance and pay policy implementations quickly learn that simply hiring employees from diverse backgrounds is a necessary but an insufficient strategy to enhance diversity and inclusion over the long term, because of difficulties in retaining women and minority employees or being able to promote them into leadership positions.

Sometimes simply communicating HR policies more effectively and increasing managers' accountability and transparency in following them can help reduce gaps. Recent research (Castilla, 2016) has demonstrated how simply posting each unit's pay raise and performance rating (transparency) increased manager accountability and ultimately helped a company achieve pay equality across gender and race. Transparency and accountability have been cited by many companies, including Deloitte (McCracken, 2000), Coca-Cola (Isdell & Bielaszka-DuVernay, 2008), and Lilly (Fitzgerald, 2018), as one of the reasons why they have succeeded in their diversity and inclusion efforts.

- **Increase cultural and structural supports to help minority groups advance.**
Dobbin & Kalev (2016) conducted a study and concluded that a key reason why many companies' early efforts to increase diversity through hiring practices did not work well is that the firms did not provide new employees with enough positive cultural support. Although many employers had aggressive recruitment policies and stated on paper that they valued diversity, they also often did not make any other major structural changes – defined as changes in formal human-resources policies or organizational practices to address gaps in supporting the diverse needs of women and minority employees. Examples include offering work-life supports for working mothers and fathers or implementing leadership-development programs to help minorities have equal access to mentors. Many minorities were "solos" or "firsts" in leadership roles who needed and valued increased social support to foster inclusion yet were not receiving this support.

- **Shift the organizational climate to increase support for diversity and inclusion by increasing representational and cultural support of underrepresented groups at all levels of the firm.**
Another way to address decoupling between formal policy and actual practice is to identify gaps between increasing diversity representation at lower levels in the workforce and the actions needed

to align prevailing cultures and structures at all levels of the firm to support inclusion. Sometimes organizations make a structural demographic change to increase the diversity of the gender and racial-ethnic composition of the workforce through hiring, but leaders then do not make a sufficient effort to help members culturally develop consensus that they value the talents diverse employees bring. Thus, decoupling can occur not only in not adding practices to address diverse employees' needs, as noted in the examples above, but also in gaps between HR diversity policies and leadership cultural systems to support an increasingly diverse workforce. An example of this problem is provided by a study conducted by Kossek and colleagues (Kossek, Markel, & McHugh, 2003) of a university's efforts to enhance diversity through increased diversity recruitment efforts. Although the researchers found that the employer successfully changed the race and sex composition over an eight-year period to significantly increase women's representation by 36 percent and minority representation by 41 percent, employees in departments with the greatest increase in workforce diversity did not have consensus that this was a positive change and did not perceive an inclusive climate. A reason for this is that diversity practices that focus mainly on "hiring diversity" without additional action to change the culture to increase all members' appreciation of diversity are likely to fail. Such diversity efforts focus on creating structural demographic change at the lower levels of the organization without making concomitant changes to foster supportive group norms and positive climates for inclusion and diversity across the organization. If women and minorities are not well-represented at the top of the firm, competitive dynamics occur between underrepresented groups at lower levels of the firm. Hiring diversity as a primary diversity enhancement objective is an insufficient organizational change strategy due to decoupling between HR recruitment policy and inclusion climates that value women and minorities as leaders and contributors. This gap simply leads to frustration, stalled careers, and turnover.

- **Conduct training and education on implicit bias, and evaluate implicit bias in prevailing policies and practices.**

What other actions can organizations take? Deloitte has been a leader in *conducting implicit bias training and audits.* Realizing that women employees were leaving the company at a higher rate than their male counterparts, Deloitte created a task force to find out why women were leaving the company and what was needed to retain them. Deloitte found many examples of bias in how women and men were being evaluated and perceived. They created workshop scenarios showing that while women tended to be evaluated based on performance, men tended to be evaluated on potential, and that this caused women with higher performance ratings to leave because they were not being promoted or faced lagging pay levels. They also developed scenarios where men and women parents might each come in late in the morning and had trainees discuss different gendered assumptions. Deloitte also examined common company social events such as golf weekends that essentially excluded women. The company required units to conduct reviews to make sure women were getting their fair share of top assignments compared to men with similar skills. These new policies and Deloitte's efforts paid off, resulting in an increase in women partners, similar turnover rates for women and men, and cost savings of millions of dollars in recruiting, hiring, and training (McCracken, 2000). Today, Deloitte is still very successful in diversity management, having been ranked twelfth in diversity and tenth nationally in mentoring in 2017 by DiversityInc, an organization with "the mission to bring education and clarity to business benefits of diversity."

- **Involve senior managers in diversity and inclusion efforts to mentor leaders at all levels of the firm.**

A third type of decoupling to address is *the gap between formal policy design that exists on paper and actual implementation.* After reviewing the diversity policies of more than 700 companies (Dobbin & Kalev,

2016; Kalev et al., 2006), researchers emphasized the importance of having line managers be committed to implementing the policies and ensuring their success. Dobbin and Kalev (2016) recommend getting managers to be engaged in and care about the success of diversity activities as a critical foundational strategy. They noted that when senior managers and leaders get more involved in recruitment and mentoring, companies get good results in retaining employees. For example, after five years of implementing a formal mentoring program, Coca-Cola retained 100 percent of Asian, 81 percent of African-American, and 73 percent of Latino employees who were in the program (Isdell & Bielaszka-DuVernay, 2008).

REFERENCES

Ayman, R., & Korabik, K. (2010). Leadership: Why gender and culture matter. *American Psychologist, 65*(3), 157–70. https://doi.org/10.1037/a0018806.

Bargh, J.A., & Chartrand, T.L. (1999). The unbearable automaticity of being. *American Psychologist, 54*(7), 462–79. https://doi.org/10.1037/0003-066X.54.7.462.

Becker, M., Vignoles, V.L., Owe, E., Brown, R., Smith, P.B., Easterbrook, M., et al. (2012). Culture and the distinctiveness motive: Constructing identity in individualistic and collectivistic contexts. *Journal of Personality and Social Psychology, 102*(4), 833–55. https://doi.org/10.1037/a0026853.

Brewer, M.B. (1999). The psychology of prejudice: Ingroup love or outgroup hate? *Journal of Social Issues, 55*(3), 429–44. https://doi.org/10.1111/0022-4537.00126.

Brimhall, K.C., Mor Barak, M.E., Hurlburt, M., McArdle, J.J., Palinkas, L., & Henwood, B. (2017). Increasing workplace inclusion: The promise of leader-member exchange. *Human Service Organizations: Management, Leadership & Governance, 41*(3), 222–39. https://doi.org/10.1080/23303131.2016.1251522.

Bromley, P., & Powell, W.W. (2012). From smoke and mirrors to walking the talk: Decoupling in the contemporary world. *The Academy of Management Annals*, 6(1), 483–530. https://doi.org/10.5465/19416520 .2012.684462.

Castilla, E.J. (2016, Summer). Achieving meritocracy in the workplace. *MIT Sloan Management Review*, 35–41.

Chen, X.-P., He, W., & Weng, L.-C. (2018). What is wrong with treating followers differently? The basis of leader-member exchange differentiation matters. *Journal of Management*, 44(3), 946–71. https://doi.org/10.1177/0149206315598372.

Cox, T.H. (1993). *Cultural diversity in organizations: Theory, research, and practice*. San Francisco: Barrett-Koehler.

Crawford. B. (2019, May 10). Leading differently. Retrieved from https://leadingdifferently.com/2018/05/10/diversity-vs-inclusion/.

Davidson, M.N., & Ferdman, B.M. (2001). A matter of difference – diversity and inclusion: What difference does it make? *Industrial-Organizational Psychologist*, 39(2), 36–3. https://doi.org/10.1037/e576912011-006.

DeRue, D.S., & Wellman, N. (2009). Developing leaders via experience: The role of developmental challenge, learning orientation, and feedback availability. *Journal of Applied Psychology*, 94(4), 859. https://doi.org/10.1037/a0015317.

DiTomaso, N., Post, C., & Parks-Yancy, R. (2007). Workforce diversity and inequality: Power, status, and numbers. *Annual Review of Sociology*, 33, 473–501. https://doi.org/10.1146/annurev.soc.33.040406.131805.

DiversityInc. (n.d.). No. 12 Deloitte. Retrieved from https://www.diversityinc.com/deloitte-2017.

Dobbin, F., & Kalev, A. (2016). Why diversity programs fail. *Harvard Business Review*, 21. Retrieved from https://hbr.org/2016/07/why-diversity-programs-fail.

Dragoni, L., Tesluk, P.E., Russell, J.E., & Oh, I.-S. (2009). Understanding managerial development: Integrating developmental assignments, learning orientation, and access to developmental opportunities in predicting managerial competencies. *Academy of Management Journal,* 52(4), 731–43. https://doi.org/10.5465/amj.2009.43669936.

Duffy, M.K., Ganster, D.C., & Pagon, M. (2002). Social undermining in the workplace. *Academy of Management Journal, 45*(2), 331–51. https://doi.org/10.5465/3069350.

Dwertmann, D., Nishii, L.H., & van Knippenberg, D. (2016). Disentangling the fairness & discrimination and synergy perspectives on diversity climate: Moving the field forward. *Journal of Management, 42*(5), 1136–68. https://doi.org/10.1177/0149206316630380.

Eagly, A.H., & Karau, S.J. (2002). Role congruity theory of prejudice toward female leaders. *Psychological Review, 109*(3), 573. https://doi.org/10.1037/0033-295X.109.3.573.

Eden, D. (1992). Leadership and expectations: Pygmalion effects and other self-fulfilling prophecies in organizations. *Leadership Quarterly, 3*(4), 271–305. https://doi.org/10.1016/1048-9843(92)90018-B.

Ely, R.J., & Thomas, D.A. (2001). Cultural diversity at work: The effects of diversity perspectives on work group processes and outcomes. *Administrative Science Quarterly, 46*(2), 229–73. https://doi.org/10.2307/2667087.

Ensari, N., & Miller, N. (2005). Prejudice and intergroup attributions: The role of personalization and performance feedback. *Group Processes & Intergroup Relations, 8*(4), 391–410. https://doi.org/10.1177/1368430205056467.

Ensari, N., & Miller, N. (2006). The application of the personalization model in diversity management. *Group Process & Intergroup Relations, 9*(4), 589–607. https://doi.org/10.1177/1368430206067679.

Farh, J.-L., Hackett, R.D., & Liang, J. (2007). Individual-level cultural values as moderators of perceived organizational support–employee outcome relationships in China: Comparing the effects of power distance and traditionality. *Academy of Management Journal, 50*(3), 715–29. https://doi.org/10.5465/amj.2007.25530866.

Fitzgerald, J. (2018, October). How Lilly is getting more women into leadership positions. *Harvard Business Review.* Retrieved from

https://hbr.org/2018/10/how-lilly-is-getting-more-women-into
-leadership-positions.

Ford, L.R., & Seers, A. (2006). Relational leadership and team climates: Pitting differentiation versus agreement. *The Leadership Quarterly*, 17(3), 258–70. https://doi.org/10.1016/j.leaqua.2006.02.005.

Gerstner, C.R., & Day, D.V. (1997). Meta-analytic review of leader-member exchange theory: Correlates and construct issues. *Journal of Applied Psychology*, 82(6), 827–44. https://doi.org/10.1037/0021-9010.82.6.827.

Green, T.K., & Kalev, A. (2008). Discrimination-reducing measures at the relational level. *Hastings Law Journal*, 59, 1435–57.

Greenhaus, J.H., Parasuraman, S., & Wormley, W. (1990). Organizational experiences and career success of black and white managers. *Academy of Management Journal*, 33(1), 64–86. https://doi.org/10.5465/256352.

Gully, S.M., Devine, D.J., & Whitney, D.J. (1995). A meta-analysis of cohesion and performance: Effects of level of analysis and task interdependence. *Small Group Research*, 26(4), 497–520. https://doi.org/10.1177/1046496495264003.

Harter, J.K., Schmidt, F.L., & Keyes, C.L. (2003). Well-being in the workplace and its relationship to business outcomes: A review of the Gallup studies. In C.L.M. Keyes & J. Haidt (Eds.), *Flourishing: Positive psychology and the life well-lived*, 205–24. Washington, DC: American Psychological Association. http://dx.doi.org/10.1037/10594-009.

Heathfield, S.M. (2019, 19 May). 10 fun icebreakers games for any work event. *The Balance Careers*. Retrieved from https://www.thebalancecareers.com/top-ice-breakers-1918426.

Heilman, M.E. (2001). Description and prescription: How gender stereotypes prevent women's ascent up the organizational ladder. *Journal of Social Issues*, 57(4), 657–74. https://doi.org/10.1111/0022-4537.00234.

Heilman, M.E., Block, C.J., & Lucas, J.A. (1992). Presumed incompetent: Stigmatization and affirmative action efforts. *Journal of Applied Psychology*, 77(4), 536–44. https://doi.org/10.1037/0021-9010.77.4.536.

Hewlin, P.F. (2003). And the award for best actor goes to ... : Facades of conformity in organizational settings. *Academy of Management Review, 28*(4), 633–42. https://doi.org/10.5465/amr.2003.10899442.

Hewlin, P.F. (2009). Wearing the cloak: Antecedents and consequences of creating facades of conformity. *Journal of Applied Psychology, 94*(3), 727–41. https://doi.org/10.1037/a0015228.

Hofstede, G., Hofstede, G.J., & Minkov, M. (1991). *Cultures and organizations: Software of the mind* (Vol. 2). London: McGraw-Hill.

Holvino, E., Ferdman, B.M., & Merrill-Sands, D. (2004). Creating and sustaining diversity and inclusion in organizations: Strategies and approaches. In M.S. Stockdale & F.J. Crosby (Eds.), *The psychology and management of workplace diversity*, 245–76. Malden: Blackwell Publishing.

Ibarra, H., Ely, R.J., & Kolb, D.M. (2013, 1 September). Women rising: The unseen barriers. *Harvard Business Review*. Retrieved from https://hbr.org/2013/09/women-rising-the-unseen-barriers.

Isdell, N., & Bielaszka-DuVernay, C. (2008). How Coca-Cola built strength on diversity. *Harvard Management Update*, U08048. Retrieved from diversitybdf.forumprofi.de/download/file.php?id=27.

Kahn, W.A. (1990). Psychological conditions of personal engagement and disengagement at work. *The Academy of Management Journal, 33*(4), 692–724. https://doi.org/10.2307/256287.

Kalev, A., Dobbin, F., & Kelly, E. (2006). Best practices or best guesses? Assessing the efficacy of corporate affirmative action and diversity policies. *American Sociological Review, 71*(4), 589–617. https://doi.org/10.1177/000312240607100404.

Kanter, R.M. (1977). Some effects of proportions on group life. In P.P. Rieker & E. Carmen (Eds.), *The Gender Gap in Psychotherapy*, 53–78. Boston: Springer.

Kossek, E.E., Markel, K., & McHugh, P. (2003). Increasing diversity as an HRM change strategy. *Journal of Organizational Change Management, 16*(3), 328–52. https://doi.org/10.1108/09534810310475550.

Kossek, E., Pichler, S., Bodner, T., & Hammer, L. (2011). Workplace social support and work-family conflict: A meta-analysis clarifying the influence of general and work-family specific supervisor and organizational support. *Personnel Psychology, 64*(2), 289–313. https://doi.org/10.1111/j.1744-6570.2011.01211.x.

Liang, J., Farh, C.I., & Farh, J.L. (2012). Psychological antecedents of promotive and prohibitive voice: A two-wave examination. *Academy of Management Journal, 55*(1), 71–92. https://doi.org/10.5465/amj.2010.0176.

Macey, W.H., & Schneider, B. (2008). The meaning of employee engagement. *Industrial and Organizational Psychology, 1*(1), 3–30. https://doi.org/10.1111/j.1754-9434.2007.0002.x.

Macey, W.H., Schneider, B., Barbera, K.M., & Young, S.A. (2009). *Employee engagement: Tools for analysis, practice, and competitive advantage.* West Sussex, UK: John Wiley & Sons Ltd.

McCracken, D.M. (2000, November–December). Winning the talent war for women: Sometimes it takes a revolution. *Harvard Business Review,* 159–64.

Nishii, L.H. (2011). Eliminating the experiential differences that divide diverse groups through climate for inclusion. Paper presented in M. Thomas-Hunt (Chair), *Managing status differentials in demographically diverse groups.* Symposium conducted at the annual conference of the Academy of Management in San Antonio, TX.

Nishii, L.H. (2013). The benefits of climate for inclusion for gender-diverse groups. *Academy of Management Journal, 56*(6), 1754–74. https://doi.org/10.5465/amj.2009.0823.

Nishii, L.H. (2015). *Climate for inclusion: A program of research.* Presentation at the Rotterdam School of Management, the Netherlands.

Nishii, L.H. (2017). *Fostering and benefiting from inclusive team climates.* Presentation at the 25th Annual Kravis De-Roulet Conference on Inclusive leadership, Claremont McKenna College, CA.

Nishii, L.H., & Bruyere, S.M. (2013). *Inside the workplace: Case studies of factors influencing engagement of people with disabilities.* State of the Science Conference on Employer Practices Related to Employment Outcomes among Individuals with Disabilities (funded by the

U.S. Department of Education National Institute on Disability and
Rehabilitation Research), Washington, DC.

Nishii, L.H., Khattab, J., Shemla, M., & Paluch, R. (2018). A multi-level
process model for understanding diversity practice effectiveness.
Academy of Management Annals, 12(1), 37–82. https://doi.org/10.5465
/annals.2016.0044.

Nishii, L.H., & Langevin, A. (2009). *Climate for inclusion: Unit predictors and
outcomes.* Paper presented at the annual conference of the Academy of
Management in Chicago, IL.

Nishii, L.H., Leroy, H., & Simons, T.L. (2014). A behavioral integrity lens
on climate research. Paper presented in T.L. Simons (Chair), *Behavioral
integrity – Perceived word-action alignment – as a driver of power of words.*
Symposium conducted at the annual conference of the Academy of
Management, Philadelphia, PA.

Nishii, L.H., Leroy, H., & Veestraeten, M. (2014). Inclusive leadership.
Paper presented in B. Chung (Chair), *Moving from diversity to inclusion:
New directions in inclusion research.* Annual SIOP conference, Honolulu,
HI.

Nishii, L.H., & Mayer, D.M. (2009). Do inclusive leaders help to reduce
turnover in diverse groups? The moderating role of leader-member
exchange in the diversity to turnover relationship. *Journal of Applied
Psychology, 94*(6), 1412–26. https://doi.org/10.1037/a0017190.

Nishii, L.H., McAlpine, K.M., Rubineau, B., & Bruyere, S. (2015). *A social
networks approach for understanding the relationship between inclusive
workgroup climates and group outcomes.* Paper presented at the 8th
Annual People and Organizations Conference, The Wharton School,
University of Pennsylvania.

Page, S.E. (2007). Making the difference: Applying a logic of diversity.
Academy of Management Perspectives, 21(4), 6–20. https://doi.org
/10.5465/amp.2007.27895335.

Phillips, K.W., Dumas, T.L., & Rothbard, N.P. (2018, March–April).
Diversity and authenticity. *Harvard Business Review.* Retrieved from
https://hbr.org/2018/03/diversity-and-authenticity.

Polzer, J.T., Milton, L.P., & Swann, W.B. (2002). Capitalizing on diversity: Interpersonal congruence in small work groups. *Administrative Science Quarterly, 47*(2), 296–324. https://doi.org/10.2307/3094807.

Ragins, B.R. (2008). Disclosure disconnects: Antecedents and consequences of disclosing invisible stigmas across life domains. *Academy of Management Review, 33*(1), 194–215. https://doi.org/10.5465/amr.2008.27752724.

Ragins, B.R., & Sundstrom, E. (1989). Gender and power in organizations: A longitudinal perspective. *Psychological Bulletin, 105*(1), 51. https://doi.org/10.1037/0033-2909.105.1.51.

Ridgeway, C.L. (1991). The social construction of status value: Gender and other nominal characteristics. *Social Forces, 70*(2), 367–86. https://doi.org/10.2307/2580244.

Ridgeway, C.L., & Correll, S.J. (2006). Consensus and the creation of status beliefs. *Social Forces, 85*(1), 431–53. https://doi.org/10.1353/sof.2006.0139.

Roberson, Q.M. (2006). Disentangling the meanings of diversity and inclusion in organizations. *Group and Organization Management, 31*(2), 212–36. https://doi.org/10.1177/1059601104273064.

Schug, J., Yuki, M., & Maddux, W. (2010). Relational mobility explains between- and within-culture differences in self-disclosure to close friends. *Psychological Science, 21*(10), 1471–78. https://doi.org/10.1177/0956797610382786.

Shore, L.M., Randel, A.E., Chung, B.G., Dean, M.A., Holcombe Ehrhart, K., & Singh, G. (2011). Inclusion and diversity in work groups: A review and model for future research. *Journal of Management, 37*(4), 1262–89. https://doi.org/10.1177/0149206310385943.

Summers, I., Coffelt, T., & Horton, R.E. (1988). Work-group cohesion. *Psychological Reports, 63*(2), 627–36. https://doi.org/10.2466/pr0.1988.63.2.627.

Tajfel, H., & Turner, J.C. (1986). The social identity theory of intergroup behavior. In S. Worchel & W. Austin (Eds.), *Psychology of intergroup relations,* 7–24. Chicago: Nelson Hall.

Tsui, A.S., & O'Reilly, C.A. (1989). Beyond simple demographic effects: The importance of relational demography in superior-subordinate dyads. *Academy of Management Journal, 32*(2), 402–23. https://doi.org/10.5465/256368.

van Knippenberg, D., De Dreu, C.K., & Homan, A.C. (2004). Work group diversity and group performance: An integrative model and research agenda. *Journal of Applied Psychology, 89*(6), 1008. https://doi.org/10.1037/0021-9010.89.6.1008.

Williams, K.Y., & O'Reilly, C.A. (1998). Demography and diversity in organizations: A review of 40 years of research. In B.M. Staw & L.L. Cummings (Eds.), *Research in organizational behavior,* Vol. 20: 77–140. Greenwich, CT: JAI.

3

MENTORING AND OTHER STRATEGIES FOR ADVANCING WOMEN'S CAREERS

A mentor is someone who allows you to see the hope inside yourself.
                                    – Oprah Winfrey (Winfrey, 2002)

What the Research Tells Us: Glass-Ceiling Chisels

BELLE ROSE RAGINS

You've Come a Long Way, Baby

I would like to examine the progress women have made toward achieving positions of leadership. But how far have we really come over the past thirty years? Thirty years ago, we were told that we have come a long way. In fact, some of you may remember the 1980s Virginia Slims ad, "You've come a long way, baby." My response then and now is, "We haven't come far enough, and quit calling me baby." Let me be the first to take you back in time and share my story. We can decide together whether we have come a long way or not.

Thirty years ago, I was a bright-eyed, newly minted PhD, interviewing for my very first academic position at the National Academy of Management meeting. The Academy of Management is the primary professional association for management professors in the United States, and it hosts a job-placement service for academics.

Things were really different back then. Instead of being interviewed in a public setting, job candidates were interviewed in the interviewer's hotel room. You would line up in the hallway and wait to be escorted into the room. Because there were so few women in business schools back then, the interviewers were inevitably men. Now you have to understand, the one thing my mother always told me was, "Belle, never, *ever*, *ever* go into a hotel room with a strange man. Bad things happen to girls who get lured into these situations." So I'm standing in the hallway, and the hair is rising on the back of my neck, and I can almost hear the defense attorney's haughty question, "So, Ms. Ragins, what exactly were you thinking going into that room with two strange men?" Yet, there I was. No choice. That was the way things were done. You walk through the door into that small hotel room – two beds – maybe a chair or two. If the men were considerate, they would offer you the chair, but all too often, they would take the chair, which meant that you were interviewed, for your first professional position as an academic, sitting on a bed. If you were lucky, the room was made up, but if you had a morning interview, the beds were unmade. Professors do not have the corner market on tidiness, and I remember having to answer a question about my dissertation while desperately trying to avoid staring at a pair of men's underwear peeking out from under the bed. The more I tried to look away, the more my eyes were drawn to it.

What is interesting about all of this is that *no one questioned the practice*. These were management professors, responsible for teaching future managers best practices on interviewing and hiring, interviewing young women in hotel rooms. Did these male professors think about how these young women felt being interviewed on an unmade bed in a strange hotel room by two older men? I do not think so. What is even more disturbing is that the Academy of Management, our primary professional association, supported this practice. They sponsored the job placement service. No one questioned it. It was how you interviewed for a job at the academy. As to the women, we bucked up and tried to take it in stride. It was a rite of passage, another hurdle to jump. We did not want to raise a fuss, to appear too sensitive or too demanding. It was just the way things were – the status quo. You have to wonder about what we accept now as "the status quo." What stories will we tell thirty years from now about today? Given the glass ceiling and inflexible workplaces, I am sure that we will have plenty of stories to tell in the future.

I wish my story ended there, but it does not. I landed my first academic position at a university, where I was one of *two* female faculty members, not just in the Management Department but in the entire School of Business. We stood out. We were an oddity, and we were both assistant professors. A short time after I started my job, a senior faculty member confided in me something his colleague had said in a department hiring meeting. The colleague was asked to report back on the interviews he had conducted at the academy meeting so the department (all men) could decide on which candidates to invite for a campus interview. When he got to me, this colleague mused that he could not help wondering *"if there was anything behind those pretty blue eyes of hers."* He did not talk about my awards, or my publications, or my qualifications, or even my interview performance. He talked about my blue eyes. I became very angry when I heard about it. First of all, my eyes are green, not blue; but what really got to me was that despite all of my hard work and preparation, years of training, and academic track record (armfuls of awards, top-tier publications, sterling grades, and recommendations), my new colleague questioned my competence and intelligence simply because of the color of my eyes. I did not have a name for it back then, but I knew it was gendered. He would never question the competence of a male candidate because of his eye color. Even though I had passed the bedroom test, I was now faced with a new set of challenges from colleagues who would determine whether I received tenure at this institution. I remind you that, at the time, we were told and believed that we had "come a long way." How far had we really come? I thanked that faculty member for sharing this information with me. I thought he was supportive and on my side, telling me about our sexist co-workers. Looking back, though, I realize that none of the men in the room, including that faculty member, confronted the offender on his blatantly sexist comment. I wonder if any of them would now. The problem is not just the comment; it is the silence that follows.

I believe these attitudes are still here. Women are still judged as incompetent until proven otherwise. People may not say it out loud, but they still believe that women are just not as good as men and that they are just not cut out to be leaders. We are seen as too nurturing or too cold, too sensitive, or not sensitive enough. Moreover, there is this basic lack of respect. We are talked over in meetings. Our ideas are either discounted or hijacked. We are still judged by the way we look and how we dress, the size of our ankles, and the color of our eyes. Sometimes these attitudes are not even conscious, but they are there. I believe this is one of the key reasons for the persistence of the glass ceiling. It is not about the pipeline. It's not about women not being qualified or not having the right type of experience. These excuses do not work anymore. The glass ceiling persists because of fundamental questioning of women's competence and ability for no other reason than their gender.

When we look at the current state of the glass ceiling, it is abysmal. As the Catalyst report shows, we have not seen much progress over the past twenty years. The percentage of female CEOs in Fortune 500 companies rose from 0 percent in 1995 to only 4.8 percent in 2014, which means that we have about 24 female CEOs out of 500 (Catalyst, 2013a). In fact, a recent *New York Times* article acknowledged that there are more CEOs named John than there are female CEOs in all of the S&P 1500 companies put together (Wolfers, 2015). When we look at board seats, the percentage of Fortune 500 board seats held by women moved from 9.6 percent in 1995 to 14.7 percent in 2005 but has flat-lined since (Catalyst, 2006, 2007, 2008, 2009, 2010, 2011, 2012,

2013b). Glaciers move faster. This is not a "pipeline" issue. We need to acknowledge the role of gender stereotypes, which fuel damaging perceptions, attributions, and behaviors. Although most men know better than to openly say "Is there anything behind those pretty blue eyes of hers?," many may still think it. Sometimes they may not even be aware of it, but the perception is still there.

This creates an uphill battle for female managers. Women have to walk a tightrope, a fine line. You cannot be too assertive, or you will be seen as aggressive. You cannot show any emotion, or you will be seen as weak, but if you do not show emotion, you are the "Iron Maiden" and can be criticized for being not feminine enough. Female leaders are scrutinized and deal with stereotypes, implicit biases, micro-inequities, and blatant discrimination. They face expectations reflecting the "double-bind of the female manager" and "think manager, think male" (Schein, Mueller, Lituchy, & Liu, 1996). So if they act like "managers" (strong, assertive, take charge), they are not seen as feminine, but if they conform to female stereotypes (warm, nurturing, supportive), then they are not seen as management material. This constant battle erodes our self-esteem and energy. We begin to doubt ourselves. We are told to "lean in," "bend over," and "stay home." We are somehow blamed for all of this. This needs to change – but how do you change attitudes? It is a long process that must start at a very young age. In the meantime, we need support. We need relationships, not just any type of relationship. We need effective mentoring relationships. This is a chisel that can help us break through the glass ceiling.

Mentoring Works

When we look at people who are effective leaders – those who have made it to the top – they share one thing in common. They have mentors. We like to think that people climb the mountain to the top of the organization on their own. Nice story, but the reality is that no one does it on their own. People have mentors. In fact, research has shown that most of the people who reach positions of power in organizations had mentors who helped them along the way. It is important to remember that mentors do more than just help you climb the mountain or reach the summit. They give you support and affirmation. They encourage you to do the things you think you cannot do, stand by your side when you stretch for those goals, and help you get back on your feet if you fall. This is so critical for women and people of color. Mentors can help us deal with the everyday micro-inequities, the innuendos, the slights and slurs, and the questioning of competence based purely on gender or race. Sometimes we call this "death by a thousand paper cuts," but often the cuts go much deeper. They cut to the quick, our self-esteem. Mentors can support our careers, build our self-esteem, and help us navigate the political terrain and battlefield of the workplace.

As researchers, we know that mentoring works. We have been studying it for a very long time, and the findings are clear and consistent. When we compare those who have mentors with those who do not, those with mentors experience more positive outcomes across compensation, advancement, promotion, job satisfaction, job involvement, performance, learning and organizational socialization, organizational commitment, turnover intentions, organizational citizenship behaviors, career satisfaction, and self-efficacy (Allen, Eby, Poteet, Lentz, & Lima, 2004; Eby, Allen, Evans, Ng, & DuBois, 2008; Dougherty & Dreher, 2007). Mentoring is also positively related to health and well-being, including psychological stress, role strain, and work-life balance (Allen et al., 2004; Eby et al., 2008; Dougherty & Dreher, 2007) and organizational effectiveness (Allen, Smith, Mael, O'Shea, & Eby, 2009).

Mentoring may also buffer employees from the negative effects of a discriminatory workplace. My colleagues and I (Ragins, Ehrhardt, Lyness, Murphy, & Capman, 2017) examined whether mentors can buffer employees from the negative effects of ambient racial discrimination at work. Ambient racial discrimination is witnessing or being aware of racial discrimination aimed at others in the workplace. It's also called the "second-hand smoke effect" (Chrobot-Mason, Ragins, & Linnehan, 2013). Ambient racial discrimination is a stressor, and we found that it predicted insomnia, physical symptoms of stress at work, and stress-related absenteeism. We also found that employees who were exposed to ambient racial discrimination had less commitment to their organization than those who did not have this exposure. We found this toxic effect for both white employees and employees of color. However, those who had mentors experienced fewer of these adverse effects than those who did not. Mentors buffered employees from the negative effects of ambient racial discrimination at work. We dug deeper and found that mentors did this by exhibiting "holding behaviors" in their relationships. Holding behaviors provide an "arms-around experience" of support, affirmation, and perspective. The relationship becomes a safe haven where people can share their concerns and experiences without fear of judgment or retribution. We found that supervisors and close co-workers also exhibited holding behaviors in their relationships, but their holding behaviors were not effective. They were unable to buffer employees from the negative effects of ambient racial discrimination. This tells us that mentoring relationships are very special and unique relationships. Close co-workers and managers cannot take the place of a mentor.

Gender, Mentoring, and Glass-Ceiling Effects

Mentors are particularly important for women and can help them deal with gender-related challenges in the workplace. We know that women with mentors do better than those without mentors (O'Brien, Biga, Kessler, & Allen, 2010; Ragins, 1999; McKeen & Bujaki, 2007). Women report more barriers to getting a mentor than men (Ragins & Cotton, 1991). Consequently, they have to work harder to actually get a mentor. While research shows that women are as likely as men to receive *career functions* from their mentors, such as sponsorship, protection, buffering, and visibility, they are less likely to receive psychosocial functions from their mentors, such as support, counseling, friendship, and role modeling (Ragins, 1989, 1999, 2002, 2007; Ragins & Cotton, 1991, 1993, 1999). This is an important finding, as these psychosocial functions are critical forms of support for female leaders facing gender-related barriers to advancement. They need support, friendship, and affirmation from their mentors, but they are less likely than their male counterparts to get it.

One reason why women receive less psychosocial support than men is because of the likely gender composition of dyads in mentoring relationships. Women are more likely than men to be in cross-gender mentoring relationships. In other words, while men are likely to have mentors of the same gender, women are more likely to have a mentor of the opposite gender. When you are in a mentoring relationship with someone of the same gender, there is more comfort, more role modeling, and perhaps less sexual tension or apprehension about what others may think or say about your relationship. It is easier to invite a mentor to go out for a beer after work if that mentor is the same gender as you because there is less to worry about. You do not have to second-guess or worry as much, and the mentor may also feel more comfortable with you. That is a real barrier for women, and this barrier is due to the glass ceiling.

The glass ceiling means that the higher up you go in organizations, the more likely you are to find men. Mentors are, by definition, senior individuals who are at higher levels in the organization. This means that young male protégés have a large pool of potential same-gender mentors in their organization to pick from, but female protégés do not. They have a much smaller pool of potential female mentors at higher ranks, and these higher-ranking women are often swamped with requests for mentoring from the throngs of lower-ranking women in their organization. Moreover, they are dealing with their own challenges: they are often the only female in an all-male environment and are expected to serve on every committee and task force on gender. On top of that, they are expected to mentor the younger women and may be seen as "Queen Bees" if they do not. They are held to a higher standard than their male counterparts.

Women need not only mentoring relationships but high-quality relationships. Mentoring relationships fall along a continuum of quality. High-quality relationships are the best, particularly when it comes to diversity. These relationships provide safe havens for developing authentic identities, thriving and surviving strategies, and an opportunity to learn about diversity (Ragins, 2012, 2016). In high-quality relationships, mentors do not just provide advice or take on the "Yoda" teacher role. They share and become vulnerable in the relationship, and this helps to create a safe haven for protégés. They can be themselves – be authentic – in the relationship. This relational authenticity allows mentors and protégés to talk about substantive and sensitive issues that are key to growth, learning, and development. This also allows them to talk about diversity, gender-related barriers to advancement, and the challenge of being authentic at work. In high-quality mentorships, you know that you are accepted for who you are and that your mentor has your back. In fact, the sharing that happens in high-quality mentorships gives both mentors and protégés an opportunity to learn about diversity at first hand, and this can be a powerful way to change attitudes.

In short, mentoring can be a chisel for the glass ceiling. It will not shatter the glass ceiling, but it can help level the playing field. To do this, we need to make the most of our mentoring relationships. We need to build high-quality mentorships and get the most from these relationships.

The Myths of Mentoring

There are several myths of mentoring that keep us from getting the most from our mentoring relationships. The first myth of mentoring is that all mentoring relationships are the same. Mentoring relationships are relationships, and no two relationships are the same. If you think about your friends, you would never say that all of your friendships are the same. You have work friends, college friends, neighborhood friends, book-club friends, and your very closest and dearest friends. You have some close friends who would do anything for you, and vice versa, friends who have your back. These friendships may be rare, but we know what they are and what they look like. We know that high-quality friendships do not happen on their own. They take sharing, time, and commitment. Like other relationships, mentoring relationships fall along a continuum of quality. Most mentoring relationships are average, but some are truly exceptional, and you can move your relationship along the continuum from marginal to magnificent. However, you cannot move from good to great unless you have a vision of what great is. Thus, the first step of developing a great mentoring relationship is to understand high-quality mentoring relationships: what they are, what they look like, and how to develop one.

The second myth of mentoring is that one mentor can do it all. This is not possible – even Superwoman has her limits. Every relationship is different. Different mentoring relationships provide different things. One mentor may be a great role model and friend but unable to sponsor you or help you get that challenging assignment. Another mentor may be a fabulous job coach but not a role model. You need to develop multiple mentoring relationships, a constellation of mentoring relationships. Some mentors may be within your organization and others outside it. Some mentors may be in your profession and others in your community. Different relationships serve different needs. You need to think about what you need and think about the relationships that can help you meet those needs.

The third myth of mentoring is that mentoring only benefits protégés: mentors also get a lot out of the relationship. As Erik Erikson points out, mentors get a sense of generativity and the satisfaction of giving back. Mentors are often at mid-life stages and have the "been-there-done-that" experience. They see their own mortality. They think about their legacy. They often get a sense of satisfaction by helping a younger person's career. They may feel as though they are getting a legacy or something even deeper. Sometimes mentors see the protégé as a younger version of themselves, which can be a problem when we are talking about White male mentors. Will a White male mentor see a Black female protégé as a younger version of himself? Not if he is thinking about this lifetime. Thus, he might be drawn to picking a protégé similar to him, which is a barrier for women and people of color. This is where consciousness raising comes in. We need to push mentors to move outside their comfort zone when selecting protégés, to motivate them to pick protégés who may be very different from them, even though their developmental needs are pushing them to pick protégés who are "Mini-mes."

The last point is about the "Queen Bee" issue I described earlier. Queen Bees are like the Miranda Priestlys of the workplace from the movie *The Devil Wears Prada*. Queen Bees are women who have made it and turn their backs on younger women who are climbing the corporate ladder. What do we call men who do not help other men? I think we just call them men. There is no such thing as a King Bee. Women are expected to help other women. That is a double standard. Men who are ambitious, who climb over other men to get to the top, may be viewed as Wall Street material, but if a woman did that, we would hear the b-word big time. Yet, there is no male equivalent for that.

Are women Queen Bees? A colleague and I (Ragins & Scandura, 1994) tested this idea in a study using a matched sample of male and female executives. We found *no support* for the Queen Bee idea. Women were not only as likely as men to be mentors; they were also more likely to report being willing to mentor and more likely to seek out other women to mentor. The Queen Bee myth undermines women. It is one more gendered expectation. Women are expected to be the mothers of the workplace, but that role is devalued. If women are competitive or aggressive, they are penalized, but this behavior is okay for men. If men are nurturing and supportive, they are viewed as Renaissance men who are extra special. Men have a wide range of acceptable behaviors, but women have to walk the tightrope.

What Organizations Can Do

There are some things organizations can do to help women. They can help women develop high-quality mentoring relationships. To start, they need to create relational mentoring cultures where mentoring is valued, recognized, and rewarded (Ragins, 2012, 2016). Organizations can also develop effective formal mentoring programs. Formal mentoring relationships are matched or assigned relationships, while informal relationships develop naturally over time. Formal mentoring relationships are not a substitute for informal relationships as they are usually of lower quality. Yet, formal relationships fall along the quality continuum. We found that high-quality formal mentoring is better than low-quality informal mentoring (Ragins, Cotton, & Miller, 2000). The most important thing is to create high-quality formal mentoring relationships. Organizations can do this by carefully selecting and training mentors, by doing a good job in matching mentors and protégés, by providing training and orientation for both members of the relationship, by monitoring the relationship, and by evaluating the program's effectiveness (Allen, Finkelstein, & Poteet, 2009; Blake-Beard, Murrell, & Thomas, 2007). In the buffer study described earlier, we found that high-quality formal mentors were able to buffer protégés from the negative effects of ambient racial discrimination at work (Ragins et al., 2017). Our other research found that protégés in high-quality formal mentorships had more positive work attitudes than those in marginal informal relationships (Ragins et al.,

2000). Formal mentoring relationships are an important resource for organizations and individuals. Unlike informal relationships, where the mentor may select a protégé on the basis of perceived similarity, formal mentoring relationships remove this barrier by offering protégés direct access to higher-ranking mentors in their organization. These diverse mentoring relationships can offer both mentors and protégés important insights about diversity and diverse experiences in organizations.

What Researchers Can Do

First, we need more research on the role of diversity in mentoring relationships. For example, we still do not know much about the experiences of women of color in mentoring relationships, and more research is needed on other aspects of diversity, such as religion, sexual orientation, and class. We also need to understand intersectionality, which is the experience of being in more than one identity group. It is also important to parse out the effects of different dimensions of diversity for women as compared to men.

Second, we need to study the dynamics of cross-gender mentoring relationships. As I mentioned earlier, women are more likely than men to be in cross-gender mentoring relationships. How do we help women make the most of these relationships? How do we help the mentor and protégé navigate gender-related issues in their relationship?

Finally, we need to learn from successful female leaders who have broken through the glass ceiling. How did she do it? What did her mentors do to help her break through the barriers to advancement? What strategies did she use? How did she develop effective mentoring relationships? What were the processes and dynamics of her relationship? Did she have multiple mentoring relationships, and if so, how did she manage them? We also need to study the mentor. How did the mentor help? What did a male mentor do to help his female protégé? What worked? What did not work? There is so much work to be done on the research front.

Conclusions

I hope this essay creates conversations and visions about the role of mentoring as a chisel for breaking the glass ceiling. Mentoring relationships can be a powerful tool for chipping away at it. However, they are not enough. We have to change attitudes. Women are not responsible for changing the attitudes and stereotypes that keep them from advancing to positions of leadership. Organizations are losing their best talent, and it is up to each and every manager and leader to speak up and intervene when they witness discrimination, marginalization, micro-aggression, or micro-inequities in the workplace. Silence is criminal. It is not up to women alone to break the glass ceiling or to change attitudes. It is everyone's responsibility.

View from Practice: Advancing Women at IBM

ROSALIA THOMAS

I work for IBM, a very remarkable company, and I really feel that way. That is why I have been at IBM for thirty-four years. I am with IBM because I want to be. I have had the opportunity to move to other organizations or other companies over my career span, but when I walked through the doors of the IBM Corporation, I found a place where my differences were looked at as opportunities within the company.

I was born in Cuba. I came to the United States when I was ten years old. I came from blue-collar parents. I am the first to graduate not only from college, but to get an advanced degree. Within the construct of IBM, I am first and foremost an "IBMer" who happens to be a Hispanic woman, who is a mother, a daughter, a wife, and an aunt, and I say that with a great deal of pride.

For those who are familiar with IBM, this company has gone through ebbs and flows throughout the years. Every business in order to survive and to be more than 100 years old has to adjust to market conditions, and that is what IBM has done over its lifetime, and it will continue to do that. For example, several years ago, we decided to take a look internally at our women leaders. We were curious about how women executives got to their positions. What were some of their opportunities? What were some of their challenges? We wanted to know this because we wanted to create programs that could help us minimize some of the challenges that these women encountered. Our plan was to provide an opportunity for our high-potential women to find mentors, find individuals within the organization that they could go talk to and learn from.

In 2013, we sent out a questionnaire to our women executives across the globe. We had 640 IBM women respond. We then identified 200 high-potential women across the world and asked them to have an in-depth, one-on-one discussion with 450 of those 640 women. After analyzing more than 270 pages of information that we received, we found something fascinating (IBM, 2013). Three major themes emerged: being visible, planning one's career, and the integration of work and life. I believe these are areas where we, as females, need to be more assertive and aggressive to be successful.

Turning to the first theme, women reported that performing well was not enough to advance unless your performance was visible to others. In an organization with more than 350,000 employees doing business in more than 170 countries, regardless of how well you think you are doing, if you do not make yourself visible to the enterprise, very few people are going to know about you. It is even more challenging to make yourself visible when your boss is in a completely different location, time zone, or even country. When opportunities present themselves, you cannot wait for somebody to tag you. To be visible, our women executives recommended building your eminence by seeking out a network and creating a career-advisory team consisting of mentors, coaches, advocates, and former and current managers.

Regarding the second theme, career planning, within IBM we have this internal culture that encourages the creation of both informal and formal mentoring relationships. Mentors are critical in an enterprise the size of mine. I have mentors who are my age, older than me, and younger than me, and they are men and women, and they are a rainbow of different nationalities. Why? Because my business requires me to do business all over the enterprise, all over the world, and so I need people that I can have an honest dialogue with, and that is what mentors bring to the table. It is a penalty-free relationship. If you have a good mentoring relationship, you should be able to talk about anything. Your mentors can guide you. If you are smart, you start with them as early as possible and you keep them. I have mentors who are now seventy-five and have been retired for ten years, and I still pick up the phone and call them. The market has changed a lot since they left the IBM Corporation, but the nuggets of wisdom and experience that they have will never change. We also need to help each other with advancement. Somebody did it for me. Actually, many people did it for me. My mentees have to commit to mentor someone. I will not take them if they do not commit. One day I will step away, and I want them to be ready to mentor the next generation of leaders.

Respondents also emphasized the importance of taking control of your career path and planning your career. Many of our women executives are advised to "find what you're passionate about, develop a game plan, and execute that plan with confidence" (IBM, 2013: 9). They also said that "if you follow your passions, the titles and promotions will follow you" (IBM, 2013: 9). The career-advisory team I mentioned earlier plays an important role in planning your career. By engaging them regularly, you can receive feedback on your performance and potential as well as career options. You also need to challenge yourself and step outside your comfort zone to expand your skills. Internal and external training, pursuing certifications or degrees, and joining professional organizations to network are some examples of how you can expand your skills. Lastly, they emphasized the importance of having a global career mindset. If feasible, taking on an assignment or a job, even a short-term one, in another country can be helpful. Mentoring someone with a different background from yours can also be helpful.

Many women agree that integrating work and personal/family life, the third main theme, was challenging. The respondents suggested: (a) not to feel guilty about decisions; (b) to delegate; (c) to create a support network; (d) to understand the resources and programs available; and (e) to seek out role models. A while ago, I competed for and got a job that would require me to travel a great deal to Latin America. At that point in my life, I had a seven-year-old child who was in emergency rooms a lot because he is severely asthmatic. My parents lived with me, and my husband was self-employed. I sat everybody around the kitchen table and asked some tough questions: "If I take this job, I'm going to be on the road a lot for the next three years. Does everybody comprehend that?" I had to tell my seven-year-old son that if I took this job, "you cannot call mommy and ask her to bring cookies for school tomorrow, because tomorrow I may be in Brazil. Do you understand that?" The creation of a support structure is critical, and your support structure must understand the long-term requirements because the entire family is impacted by your decision. The women who participated in this study all said the same thing. They had to create a support structure that worked for them, whatever that was.

The next generation of leaders needs to understand how to become visible, how to seek mentors, how to ensure that they see themselves represented in the company, and they need to know that there is a career for them. They need to understand that we know what it is like to be twenty-two, twenty-seven, thirty-five, forty-five, fifty-six, or sixty-five, because the life cycle happens to everyone.

In our corporate world today, we are finding some interesting challenges. This idea of opting out of work has received many mixed reviews. For a corporation like mine, we need a constant influx of talent, and the thought that somebody who is bright, articulate, thoughtful, creative, and innovative is opting out of the workforce scares me. We need to infuse talent into the corporation constantly. Talent comes in many forms and all age groups, and if we lose this talent, we could potentially be losing the next great idea. That would truly be a shame.

Integrating Research and Practice: Mentoring

PATRICE M. BUZZANELL

The two previous essays in this chapter have focused on how research processes and business practices might be integrated more effectively to foster women's advancement within contemporary career systems and organizational cultures that often are structured through masculine values. Although much has been written about this topic and many interventions have been devised for handling the "problem" of women's underrepresentation in top positions in all sectors, the authors, Belle Rose Ragins and Rosalia Thomas, turn our attention to the complex tensions involved and the requirement to rethink common-sense notions and propose proactive strategies for women and organizational cultures in order to develop, utilize, and display women's competencies for their own careers and for organizational competitiveness.

In this section, I reflect upon their words of wisdom to ascertain how we can engage collaboratively in the co-construction of practice that integrates experience, goals, and evidence. In doing so, my primary task is to identify the problems and opportunities around which plans can be devised. In both essays, the overarching concerns are how to create supportive relationships, networks, and organizational cultures that will help women figure out what their challenges are, who can assist them, what they need to do, and how they can accomplish their goals. The "why" underlying the need to discuss these concerns is that obstacles to women's careers and talent utilization can prevent personal work-life development and organizational success. Research often displays what to do, but the authors in this section explain how to do it. By moving from research and professional as well as personal experience to practice, we begin to generate ideas that then can be used to achieve goals. These goals center on providing productive strategies for women's advancement and enabling the assessment of strategies for revision and sustainability.

Both authors discuss the need for women to have multiple mentors with whom they can have "quality relationships" (Belle Rose Ragins) and "penalty-free" discussions (Rosalia Thomas). Both provide very specific ways to have conversations that ensure that women are able to grow, obtain feedback, and develop support for their work and personal life interests and needs. Both ground their comments in research but also in their personal and professional lives, enabling readers to understand not only what to do but with whom and how.

Recalling Belle's essay, how can practice, the "chisel for the glass ceiling," be developed to achieve the benefits that her own and others' scholarship promises? The answers to this question lie in the examples that Belle provides – trust and vulnerability, sharing of confidential information and feelings, creating reward structures that promote these activities or, at the very least, do not provide penalties for those who want to become mentors and/or mentees. She mentions that she and others can learn how to counteract spoken and non-verbal messages that diminish one's own and others' dignity and worth. In this regard, Belle inspires an approach grounded in relationships to change not only individuals' ways of doing their work but also the culture. Belle begins with concerns and derives paths for practice that resolve deeply embedded processes undermining women's advancement.

In contrast, Rosalia Thomas builds upon the foundation of an organization geared toward talent acquisition and retention as well as mentorship for all throughout its multinational structure. Starting from this position, her strategies center on how women can use that which is already available, namely the people around them and the opportunities that present themselves, or that are created by the women themselves and in concert with others. Although some might cringe at the idea of "using" others, Rosalia's strategies are based on reciprocity and growth. A woman does not mentor unless the mentee is willing to mentor others; a working mother does not ask stay-at-home mothers to cover children's activities that she cannot take on herself unless she is willing to fill in for these mothers when they could use support.

Although the research-to-practice idea is to move from empirical findings to everyday practice and structural change, we also might reverse the order, as our authors have done, and take the practices and life learning into research that better meets the needs of women as well as the needs of men.

Managerial and Organizational Actions for Mentoring and Advancing Women

ELLEN ERNST KOSSEK AND KYUNG-HEE LEE

Managerial Actions

• **Commit to developing strong managerial skills in mentoring in general and specifically to support women.**
Being a good manager of a unit's technical areas requires business skills. As a manager, you also need to develop relational skills in order to learn how to be a good mentor. An interview study (Tjan,

2017) with more than 100 leaders found that great mentors know how to *develop high-quality mentoring relationships with individuals from all backgrounds, including with women.* Reflect on how diverse your mentee network is and whether you are equally reaching out to support men and women. If you do not have a diverse network, then intentionally reach out to support women protégés (Murphy, 2019).

It is also critical to learn how to build a rapport with protégés of diverse backgrounds, a skill that should be a mentor's priority especially at the beginning of the relationship (Tjan, 2017). Stefana Hunyady at PayPal, whose mentoring program was rated as the best by InHerSight, emphasizes the importance of a rapport between mentors and protégés. In PayPal, after the mentoring pairs are matched based on a survey, the pairs have an initial meeting to determine whether they have "chemistry" with each other (Ward, 2016). Being a good listener and being able to show empathy, which Murphy (2019) defines as being able to be "attentive with both your head and your heart," are critical. Relationship building also involves being able to suspend judgment when your protégés share their own stories and cheering them on even when they present you with seemingly unrealistic or too-ambitious ideas. As a mentor, your first instinct may be to point out why the idea will not work because you want your protégé to succeed and wish to aim them in the right direction. However, the researcher's interviews with successful leaders (Tjan, 2017) urge mentors to focus on positives rather than negatives, as a way to provide ongoing social support, encouragement, value, and character socialization.

- **Actively educate yourself on gender-career-equality facts, and be ready to take action on gender issues that impact women's careers.**
Adept managers will know that women are underrepresented in the C-suite, hold less than 4 percent of Fortune 500 CEO positions,

often receive lower pay than their similarly rated male counterparts, and are slower to receive a critical first promotion to the managerial ranks (Zarya, 2016). Research shows that although women are less likely to be mentored and sponsored than men, those who have sponsors are more likely to request a challenging stretch assignment and ask for a raise (LeanIn.Org, 2019).

Showing some awareness of such career-inequality trends may also help you as a manager to bring up in conversation with a woman protégé her views on whether and how gender has impacted her career and her experiences of your organization's climate for gender inclusion. Such a dialogue will enhance your ability to provide advice on how to navigate the informal cultural career trip-wires (Murphy, 2019).

One particular issue that impacts women's careers that you should be aware of as a mentor is that women who are star employees may have substantial social capital and reputational value that may make it easier for them to advance to a higher position outside their firm than within their firm (Groysberg, 2012). Thus, high-talent women are sometimes more able to leverage themselves externally and make this talent portable to other companies. Mentoring a woman who is likely to have greater external than internal career capital may sometimes put you in a bind. You may determine that having your protégé stay at your organization or on her current career path might not be best for her career, causing loyalty discomfort if you urge her to seek external options (Tjan, 2017). Yet this may sometimes be the best for her career and your firm, if its current climate is chilly for women and unlikely to improve quickly.

- **Be aware of current cross-gender mentoring challenges in the #MeToo era and address them.**

Cross-gender mentoring, especially male mentor-female protégé relationships, faces new challenges in the #MeToo era and has led to some unintended cross-gender mentoring consequences. The *New York Times* reports that some male leaders are worried about taking on female protégés through fear that they may be accused of inappropriate behavior (Miller, 2017). You must not let fear stop you from being a mentor, however, since false accusations of sexual misconduct rarely occur – less than 2 percent of the time (Murphy, 2019). The unintended consequences of #MeToo can hinder gender career equality progress if you give in to fear. It is truly important for men, in particular, to continue to mentor women, as there are simply fewer women leaders than male leaders who can serve as mentors. If men start refusing to mentor female protégés, women will have less likelihood of obtaining mentors. To combat the unintended consequences, researchers and industry leaders are speaking out to encourage cross-gender mentoring. For example, LeanIn.Org (2019) has started a campaign called #MentorHer.

- **Ask your organization to help you design and implement safe and effective mentoring systems.**
You don't have to go it alone as a manager in setting up mentoring relationships. You can proactively ask your organization to organize formal mentoring systems with training on how to create a safe environment (Soklaridis, Zahn, Kuper, Gillis, Taylor, & Whitehead, 2018).

A safe environment begins with setting clear expectations and boundaries with your protégé. Respecting your female protégé's personal space and having her give input on meeting times and places can help foster safety. Arranging to meet in public places and scheduling lunch meetings rather than dinner meetings is also recommended (Gurchiek, 2017). For male mentors, in particular, it is important to try to tone down paternalistic gender dynamics (Tan & Porzecanski, 2018); this could include avoiding acting chivalrously (e.g., paying for meals), since chivalrous acts can be interpreted as questioning the other person's competence and creating unwanted power dynamics. It is also recommended that mentors act respectfully and avoid physical touching (Byerley, 2018). Constantly monitor yourself and apologize instantly if you make a mistake. If you are not sure whether something is appropriate or not, ask yourself, "What would HR say about it?" (Gurchiek, 2017).

Organizational Actions

- **Follow evidence-based practices to build a successful mentoring program step by step.**
High-quality mentoring does not just happen by accident. Organizations must invest resources in developing effective mentoring programs that suit their values and needs. Several researchers (Allen, Finkelstein, & Poteet, 2009) combined research findings and case studies to provide an evidence-based and practical guide to building a successful mentoring program.

The first critical step your organization should take is *to conduct a needs assessment to determine your company's mentoring needs and readiness for a mentoring program* (Allen, Finkelstein, & Poteet, 2009). For example, your organization may have realized that you need more women in leadership roles. When analyzing the reasons for the lack of women in leadership roles, you may have found that while your organization is able to attract and recruit many women, the women are having trouble moving up in the organization to leadership roles. Yet interviews with the few women leaders may reveal that mentoring was crucial in helping them advance to key leadership roles. Such trends help identify the need for a mentoring program for women.

After identifying specific mentoring needs, your organization must assess its cultural readiness and capability. Does your firm have the requisite organizational resources in place to start and maintain a successful formal mentoring program? For example, in order for a mentoring program to be successful, a training program needs to be developed for mentors and protégés; and milestones for assessing progress and outcomes need to be identified, monitored, and assessed. You may also want to identify new career and talent management structures, such as learning circles, or new ways of identifying high-potential employees and career paths for different skills and interests across functions. It is critical to note that when it comes to a mentoring program, one size does not fit all. For example, a mentoring program may not help your firm solve other business issues your firm is having, or it may not align with your business strategy.

After assessing company needs and readiness, it is critical to *establish specific program objectives that will guide you in how to structure the program and evaluate its success* (Allen, Finkelstein, & Poteet, 2009). Poorly defined program objectives are one of the reasons why mentoring programs fail (Schnieders, 2018). Your objectives will decide what types of mentoring programs to include; these can range from career mentoring, mentoring for high-potential employees, diversity mentoring, reverse mentoring (younger employees mentoring older employees for knowledge sharing), and mentoring circles (peer mentoring for collaborative learning) (Chronus, n.d.). If your objectives are to increase diversity in the organization, diversity mentoring will fit your needs. Or if your organization is having difficulty managing employee retention, career mentoring will be helpful. For example, Net-Suit, an enterprise software company, runs a mentoring program for high-performing female employees that was rated highly by InHerSight (Ward, 2016). By matching female high performers with mentors who are two levels higher in other departments, NetSuit increased female leadership by 20 percent in one year (S. Allen, 2018).

Once clear objectives are established, the employer needs to, first, *communicate to its employees that the organization is committed to supporting a mentoring program and, second, establish clear selection criteria and participation guidelines* (Allen, Finkelstein, & Poteet, 2009). Research shows that when employees perceive more support for the program, the better the outcomes (e.g., retention and advancement) will be (Parise & Forret, 2008). The specific selection criteria will depend on the mentoring program's specific objectives. If the objective is to increase women in top management, a firm will want to recruit women protégés. When selecting participants, it is important to focus on protégé and mentor characteristics that have been connected to successful outcomes. For protégés, motivation to learn has been identified as important (Colquitt, LePine, & Noe, 2000). For mentors, empathy seems to be a key characteristic (Allen, 2003). One of the most important participation guidelines to establish is whether participation in the program will be voluntary or mandatory for both protégés and mentors. While outcomes do not differ depending on whether the participation is voluntary or mandatory for protégés (Allen, Eby, & Lentz, 2006a, 2006b), the rewards for mentors are greater when they participate voluntarily (Parise & Forret, 2008).

After the participants are selected, an employer needs to carefully *match mentors and protégés* (Allen, Finkelstein, & Poteet, 2009). This often involves considering similarities between the protégé and the mentor. Similarities between a protégé and a mentor are strongly associated with better mentoring outcomes, such as satisfaction with the mentoring relationship (Allen & Eby, 2003; Turban, Dougherty, & Lee, 2002). Similarities may be based on many aspects, including demographic characteristics, work interests, non-work interests, and personality. Which similarity to focus on in matching depends on the program objectives, because matches based on different similarities may yield different outcomes. For example, personality matching encourages better relationship quality, while work interest matching is better for achieving a protégé's goals (Meikle, Poteat, Rodopman, Shockley, Yang, & Allen, 2007). Same-gender and race matching are helpful in providing role models and emotional comfort (Blake-Beard, Bayne, Crosby, & Muller, 2011; Thomas, 1990). However, because of the lack of women and racial minorities in leadership roles, gender and race matching is not always possible or practical. When matching, allowing participants to provide input is important. When protégés and mentors have some say in the match, participants report greater effectiveness of the program (Allen et al., 2006a).

The next step is to *provide formal training for protégés and mentors*, a strategy that has been demonstrated to increase the likelihood of the mentoring program's success (Allen et al., 2006a). Examples of training topics to prepare protégé and mentor participants include socialization and defining a mentoring relationship, as well as identifying program objectives and responsibilities, acceptable expectations of protégés and mentors, and possible challenges and how to overcome them. Quest Diagnostics, a diagnostic testing, information, and services company, has an exemplary training program for mentors and protégés. Their introductory workshop uses lectures, coaching, and video case studies on how to overcome challenges. Sometimes training might specifically focus on training for mentors alone – for example, in coaching skills and techniques for giving constructive feedback. Similarly, protégés might be trained separately on how to receive and use feedback (Allen, Finkelstein, & Poteet, 2009).

The last step is to *monitor and to evaluate* (Allen, Finkelstein, & Poteet, 2009). Monitoring progress helps to identify issues in the program in general and in certain relationships. Research indicates that protégés and mentors perceive monitoring as a form of support and find it helpful. Evaluating the effectiveness of the mentoring program ensures that the program is yielding the results it was intended to and helps identify areas that need change or improvement. Assessing subjective experiences of mentors and protégés (i.e., program satisfaction, relationship quality, perceived benefits, and learning) and comparing women mentors' and protégés' perceptions with those of their male counterparts is important. It is also critical to include objective measures such as retention rates and the percentage of women advancing to leadership roles, in order to ensure that the mentoring program is working as intended (Allen, Finkelstein, & Poteet, 2009).

REFERENCES

Allen, S. (2018, 13 February). Here are some incredible company initiatives that empower women. Retrieved 14 February 2019 from https://swirled.com/best-company-initiatives-for-women/.

Allen, T.D. (2003). Mentoring others: A dispositional and motivational approach. *Journal of Vocational Behavior*, *62*(1), 134–54. https://doi.org/10.1016/S0001-8791(02)00046-5.

Allen, T.D., & Eby, L.T. (2003). Relationship effectiveness for mentors: Factors associated with learning and quality. *Journal of Management*, *29*(4), 469–86. https://doi.org/10.1016/S0149-2063(03)00021-7.

Allen, T.D., Eby, L.T., & Lentz, E. (2006a). Mentorship behaviors and mentorship quality associated with formal mentoring programs: Closing the gap between research and practice. *Journal of Applied Psychology*, *91*(3), 567–78. https://doi.org/10.1037/0021-9010.91.3.567.

Allen, T.D., Eby, L.T., & Lentz, E. (2006b). The relationship between formal mentoring program characteristics and perceived program effectiveness. *Personnel Psychology*, *59*(1), 125–53. https://doi.org/10.1111/j.1744-6570.2006.00747.x.

Allen, T.D., Eby, L.T., Poteet, M.L., Lentz, E., & Lima, L. (2004). Career benefits associated with mentoring for protégés: A meta-analysis.

Journal of Applied Psychology, 89(1), 127–36. https://doi.org/10.1037 /0021-9010.89.1.127.

Allen, T.D., Finkelstein, L.M., & Poteet, M.L. (2009). *Designing workplace mentoring programs: An evidence-based approach.* Oxford: Wiley & Sons.

Allen, T.D., Smith, M.A., Mael, F.A., O'Shea, P.G., & Eby, L.T. (2009). Organization-level mentoring and organizational performance within substance abuse centers. *Journal of Management, 35*(5), 1113–28. https:// doi.org/10.1177/0149206308329969.

Blake-Beard, S., Bayne, M.L., Crosby, F.J., & Muller, C.B. (2011). Matching by race and gender in mentoring relationships: Keeping our eyes on the prize. *Journal of Social Issues, 67*(3), 622–43. https://doi.org/10.1111 /j.1540-4560.2011.01717.x.

Blake-Beard, S., Murrell, A., & Thomas, B. (2007). Unfinished business: The importance of race on understanding mentoring relationships. In B.R. Ragins & K. Kram (Eds.), *The handbook of mentoring at work: Theory, research, and practice,* 223–48. Thousand Oaks, CA: Sage.

Byerley, J.S. (2018). Mentoring in the era of #MeToo. *JAMA, 319*(12), 1199–200. https://doi.org/10.1001/jama.2018.2128.

Catalyst. (2006). 2006 Catalyst census: Fortune 500 women board directors. New York: Catalyst.

Catalyst. (2007). 2007 Catalyst census: Fortune 500 women board directors. New York: Catalyst.

Catalyst. (2008). 2008 Catalyst census: Fortune 500 women board directors. New York: Catalyst.

Catalyst. (2009). 2009 Catalyst census: Fortune 500 women board directors. New York: Catalyst.

Catalyst. (2010). 2010 Catalyst census: Fortune 500 women board directors. New York: Catalyst.

Catalyst. (2011). 2011 Catalyst census: Fortune 500 women board directors. New York: Catalyst.

Catalyst. (2012). 2012 Catalyst census: Fortune 500 women board directors. New York: Catalyst.

Catalyst. (2013a). Historical list of women CEOs of the Fortune lists: 1972–2013.

Catalyst. (2013b). 2013 catalyst census: Fortune 500 women executive officers and top earners, 1–2. New York: Catalyst.

Chrobot-Mason, D., Ragins, B., & Linnehan, F. (2013). Second hand smoke: Ambient racial harassment at work. *Journal of Managerial Psychology*, *28*(5), 470–91. https://doi.org/10.1108/JMP-02-2012-0064.

Chronus. (n.d.). The top 5 workplace mentoring program types. Retrieved 14 February 2019 from https://chronus.com/how-to-use-mentoring-in-your-workplace.

Colquitt, J.A., LePine, J.A., & Noe, R.A. (2000). Toward an integrative theory of training motivation: A meta-analytic path analysis of 20 years of research. *Journal of Applied Psychology*, *85*(5), 678–707. https://doi.org/10.1037/0021-9010.85.5.678.

Dougherty, T.W., & Dreher, G.F. (2007). Mentoring and career outcomes. In B.R. Ragins & K. Kram (Eds.), *The handbook of mentoring at work: Theory, research, and practice*, 51–93. Thousand Oaks, CA: Sage.

Eby, L.T., Allen, T.D., Evans, S.C., Ng, T., & DuBois, D.L. (2008). Does mentoring matter? A multidisciplinary meta-analysis comparing mentored and non-mentored individuals. *Journal of Vocational Behavior*, *72*(2), 254–67. https://doi.org/10.1016/j.jvb.2007.04.005.

Eddy, E., Tannenbaum, S., Alliger, G., D'Abate, C., & Givens, S. (2001). Mentoring in industry: The top 10 issues when building and supporting a mentoring program. Technical report prepared for the Naval Air Warfare Training Systems Division (Contract No. N61339–99-D-0012), Orlando, FL.

Groysberg, B. 2012. *Chasing stars: The myth of talent and the portability of performance*. Princeton, NJ: Princeton University Press.

Gurchiek, K. (2017). 7 essential guidelines for mentoring in the post-Weinstein era. Retrieved from https://www.shrm.org/resourcesandtools/hr-topics/behavioral-competencies/pages/guidelines-for-mentoring-in-the-postweinstein-era.aspx.

IBM. (2013). *Your journey to executive: Insights from IBM women executives from the 2012–2013 Advancing Women at IBM Executive Research Study*. Somers, NY: IBM.

LeanIn.Org. (2019). Men, commit to mentor women. Retrieved from https://leanin.org/mentor-her.

McKeen, C., & Bujaki, M. (2007). Gender and mentoring. In B.R. Ragins & K.E. Kram (Eds.), *The handbook of mentoring at work: Theory, research, and practice,* 197–222. Thousand Oaks, CA: Sage.

Meikle, H., Poteat, L., Rodopman, O.B., Shockley, K.M., Yang, L., & Allen, T.D. (2007). *Evaluation of the CAS formal mentoring program.* Tampa, FL: The University of South Florida.

Miller, C.C. (2017, 9 October). Unintended consequences of sexual harassment scandals. *New York Times.* Retrieved from https://www .nytimes.com/2017/10/09/upshot/as-sexual-harassment-scandals -spook-men-it-can-backfire-for-women.html.

Murphy, W. (2019, 3 March). Advice for men who are nervous about mentoring women. *Harvard Business Review.* Retrieved from https://hbr .org/2019/03/advice-for-men-who-are-nervous-about-mentoring- women.

O'Brien, K.E., Biga A., Kessler, S.R., & Allen, T.D. (2010). A meta-analytic investigation of gender differences in mentoring. *Journal of Management, 36*(2), 537–54. https://doi.org/10.1177 /0149206308318619.

Parise, M.R., & Forret, M. (2008). Formal mentoring programs: The relationship of program design and support to mentors' perceptions of benefits and costs. *Journal of Vocational Behavior, 72*(2), 225–40. https:// doi.org/10.1016/j.jvb.2007.10.011.

Ragins, B.R. (1989). Barriers to mentoring: The female manager's dilemma. *Human Relations, 42*(1), 1–22. https://doi. org/10.1177/001872678904200101.

Ragins, B.R. (1999). Gender and mentoring relationships: A review and research agenda for the next decade. In G. Powell (Ed.), *Handbook of gender and work,* 347–70. Thousand Oaks, CA: Sage.

Ragins, B.R. (2002). Understanding diversified mentoring relationships: Definitions, challenges, and strategies. In D. Clutterbuck & B.R. Ragins (Eds.), *Mentoring and diversity: An international perspective,* 23–53. Woburn, MA: Butterworth Heinemann.

Ragins, B.R. (2007). Diversity and workplace mentoring: A review and positive social capital approach. In T.D. Allen & L.T. Eby (Eds.), *Blackwell handbook of mentoring: A multiple perspectives approach,* 281–300. Oxford: Blackwell Publishing.

Ragins, B.R. (2012). Relational mentoring: A positive approach to mentoring at work. In K. Cameron and G. Spreitzer (Eds.), *The Oxford handbook of positive organizational scholarship,* 519–36. New York: Oxford University Press.

Ragins, B.R. (2016). From the ordinary to the extraordinary: High-quality mentoring relationships at work. *Organizational Dynamics, 45*(3), 228–44. https://doi.org/10.1016/j.orgdyn.2016.07.008.

Ragins, B.R., & Cotton, J.L. (1991). Easier said than done: Gender differences in perceived barriers to gaining a mentor. *Academy of Management Journal, 34*(4), 939–51. https://doi.org/10.5465/256398.

Ragins, B.R., & Cotton, J.L. (1993). Gender and willingness to mentor in organizations. *Journal of Management, 19*(1), 97–111. https://doi.org/10.1177/014920639301900107.

Ragins, B.R., & Cotton, J.L. (1999). Mentor functions and outcomes: A comparison of men and women in formal and informal mentoring relationships. *Journal of Applied Psychology, 84*(4), 529–50. https://doi.org/10.1037/0021-9010.84.4.529.

Ragins, B.R., Cotton, J.L., & Miller, J.S. (2000). Marginal mentoring: The effects of type of mentor, quality of relationship, and program design on work and career attitudes. *Academy of Management Journal, 43*(6), 1177–94. https://doi.org/10.5465/1556344.

Ragins, B.R., Ehrhardt, K., Lyness, K., Murphy, D., & Capman, J. (2017). Anchoring relationships at work: High-quality mentors and other supportive work relationships as buffers to ambient racial discrimination. *Personnel Psychology, 70*(1), 211–56. https://doi.org/10.1111/peps.12144.

Ragins, B.R., & Scandura, T.A. (1994). Gender differences in expected outcomes of mentoring relationships. *Academy of Management Journal, 37*(4), 957–71. https://doi.org/10.5465/256606.

Ragins, B.R., & Verbos, A.K. (2007). Positive relationships in action: Relational mentoring and mentoring schemas in the workplace. In J.E. Dutton & B.R. Ragins (Eds.), *Exploring positive relationships at work: Building a theoretical and research foundation*, 91–116. Mahwah, NJ: Lawrence Erlbaum Associates, Inc.

Schein, V.E., Mueller, R., Lituchy, T., & Liu, J. (1996). Think manager – think male: A global phenomenon? *Journal of Organizational Behavior*, 17(1), 33–41. https://doi.org/10.1002/(SICI)1099-1379(199601)17:1 <33::AID-JOB778>3.0.CO;2-F.

Schnieders, A. (2018, 25 June). Why workplace mentoring programs fail. Retrieved from https://www.entrepreneur.com/article/314875.

Soklaridis, S., Zahn, C., Kuper, A., Gillis, D., Taylor, V.H., & Whitehead, C. (2018). Men's fear of mentoring in the #MeToo era – What's at stake for academic medicine? *New England Journal of Medicine*, 379(23), 2270–4. https://doi.org/10.1056/NEJMms1805743.

Tan, G., & Porzecanski, K. (2018, 3 December). Wall Street rule for the #MeToo era: Avoid women at all cost. *Bloomberg*. Retrieved from https://www.bloomberg.com/news/articles/2018-12-03/a-wall-street-rule-for-the-metoo-era-avoid-women-at-all-cost.

Thomas, D.A. (1990). The impact of race on managers' experiences of developmental relationships (mentoring and sponsorship): An intra-organizational study. *Journal of Organizational Behavior*, 11(6), 479–92. https://doi.org/10.1002/job.4030110608.

Tjan, A.K. (2017, February). What the best mentors do. *Harvard Business Review*. Retrieved from https://hbr.org/2017/02/what-the-best-mentors-do.

Turban, D.B., Dougherty, T.W., & Lee, F.K. (2002). Gender, race, and perceived similarity effects in developmental relationships: The moderating role of relationship duration. *Journal of Vocational Behavior*, 61(2), 240–62. https://doi.org/10.1006/jvbe.2001.1855.

Ward, K. (2016, 5 October). These companies run mentorship programs that actually work. Retrieved 14 February 2019 from https://www

.fastcompany.com/3064292/these-companies-run-mentorship
-programs-that-actually-work.

Winfrey, O. (2002, 13 January). An interview with Oprah Winfrey on
WCVB-TV 5 News Cityline.

Wolfers, J. (2015, 2 March). Fewer women run big companies than men
named John. *The New York Times*. Retrieved from https://www
.nytimes.com/2015/03/03/upshot/fewer-women-run-big-companies
-than-men-named-john.html.

Zarya, V. (2016, 6 June). The percentage of female CEOs in the fortune 500
drops to 4%. *Fortune*. Retrieved from http://fortune.com/2016/06/06
/women-ceos-fortune-500-2016/.

4

HOW TO LEVERAGE DIVERSE TEAMS

It is hardly possible to overrate the value ... of placing human beings in contact with persons dissimilar to themselves, and with modes of thought and action unlike those with which they are familiar ... Such communication has always been, and is peculiarly in the present age, one of the primary sources of progress.

– John Stuart Mill (1848: III.17.12)

What the Research Tells Us: Claiming the Unexpected Value of Diversity

DENISE LEWIN LOYD

As a result of domestic demographics and global economic trends, organizational leaders increasingly are faced with the need to engage with and manage diversity. They are motivated to do this because of some evidence, both anecdotal and empirical, that diversity can be beneficial in groups. For example, in one study, ethnically diverse trading markets had fewer trader errors and less overpricing (Levine et al., 2014); firms with greater gender diversity on their boards had better financial performance (Campbell & Mínguez-Vera, 2008); ethnically diverse teams had more innovative (Ancona & Caldwell, 1992) and higher-quality outputs (McLeod, Lobel, &

Cox, 1996); greater gender diversity on a team was positively correlated with greater team collective intelligence (Woolley, Chabris, Pentland, Hashmi, & Malone, 2010); and greater gender and racial diversity were associated with greater sales revenue and profits in for-profit companies (Herring, 2009). On the other hand, other studies and meta-analyses have shown no benefit or negative impacts from diversity (Dobbin & Jung, 2011; van Dijk, van Engen, & van Knippenberg, 2012; van Knippenberg & Schippers, 2007). Therefore, when and why diversity can be beneficial for teams remains a question. In this essay, I first discuss the expected and unexpected value of diversity in team settings, followed by how status can influence diversity processes. I conclude the essay with a discussion of some tools that are useful to facilitate diversity in team settings.

The Value of Diversity

There is certainly something of conventional wisdom about why diversity is beneficial for teams. This account essentially suggests that diversity is beneficial because people's different experiences, information, skills, and expertise necessarily lead to different perspectives. Thus, when those who are "different" are part of the team process or discussion, it can help the members of the team consider different ideas, learn, and ultimately perform better – be more creative, innovative, and make better decisions – than when diversity is absent. This "information processing" approach to understanding diversity in teams provides an optimistic view of how diversity enhances team and organization performance (Mannix & Neale, 2005). Thus, the idea of the "value in diversity" – that diversity can benefit an organization's bottom line (Cox, Lobel, & McLeod, 1991) – is valid.

The face validity for this benefit of diversity is high, especially with cross-functional teams, and resonates in a business context. For example, we would expect a cross-functional team of engineers, doctors, patients, and lawyers (among others) to be involved in bringing a new medical device to market, with each constituent group bringing their particular perspective to bear on what attributes the device should possess. Their discussions, debates, and disagreements would arguably result in a better device than if only one perspective was considered. Scholars have argued for this benefit of diversity for organizations, suggesting that it is in their competitive interest to understand and manage characteristics like ethnic and cultural diversity effectively (Cox & Blake, 1991; Palacios, 2011). Although there are still stories like the one about a major corporation's realization within the last decade that a team of nearly all males was in charge of its feminine hygiene products brand, organizations have increasingly come to seek demographic diversity to facilitate designing and marketing products for a multicultural audience, as evidenced by the growth in multicultural marketing over the last several decades. There seems to be increased recognition that a diverse customer base can benefit from a diverse set of employees. This is predicated again on the idea that those who share the background of the group to whom the organization is trying to market a product have more relevant knowledge, experience, and expertise than those who do not. Thus, it would seem to be important to have representatives of that group at the decision-making or idea-generating table.

The Unexpected Value of Diversity

Despite a positive result of the "traditional" value of diversity story of promoting diversity in the workplace, one challenge with this perspective that is not often discussed is that it puts people in a box. In other words, it is based on and encourages seeing individuals as representatives of social categories rather than as individuals. Furthermore, taken to its extreme, it presumes that those who share some characteristic (e.g., marketers, lawyers, women) will necessarily share the same knowledge, information, and perspective and that these will necessarily differ from the knowledge, information, and perspective of those who do not share that characteristic. In other words, the women on the team will necessarily think the same thing, the men on the team will think the same thing, and the men's and women's views will necessarily differ from each other. This assumption is not entirely unfounded. A number of studies have shown that, on issues both relevant and irrelevant to the social category, people expect more agreement from those who share a salient social category with them (e.g., political affiliation, sexual orientation, or even minimal group [red group or blue group]) than from those who do not (e.g., Allen & Wilder, 1979; Chen & Kenrick, 2002). For example, in one study, Phillips and Loyd (2006) found that MBA students expected more agreement with another MBA student than with a medical student on their team about which market their team should target for a new product.

However, this is a very limiting presumption for two main reasons. First, by assuming that the "different, unique, or innovative" perspectives will come from those who are different, we are first and foremost putting high expectations and performance pressure on these "different" members of the group to provide the insight, spark, or information that the group needs to be more successful. Given that the distinguishing characteristic likely also places these individuals in the numeric minority, this pressure is on top of the pressure on their numeric minority status in the group. Second, this assumption also does a disservice to the members of the majority or dominant demographic category of the group by suggesting that their perspective is interchangeable with others who share their social category and thus is not innovative or unique. However, we know that the people who share a characteristic may disagree with one another and that those with different backgrounds may share a common perspective. The challenge is to get those different perspectives expressed and engaged with by the other members of the team.

This is the "unexpected value of diversity." The presence of diversity in a team can actually facilitate the expression of unique perspectives and more complex reasoning from all members of the team and increase engagement with those perspectives. There are several studies that demonstrate this additional value of diversity. For example, researchers (Antonio et al., 2004) assembled groups of four college students to discuss a social issue. The groups were either racially homogeneous (four Whites including the confederate) or diverse (three Whites and one Black confederate). They were asked to indicate their agreement or disagreement with a social issue and then write a pre-discussion essay in preparation for the group meeting while sitting on a table with their team members. They found that the essays written by the White students in diverse groups had more integrative complexity or demonstrated more complex thinking by considering multiple dimensions and trade-offs between different courses of action than the essays written by the White students in homogeneous groups.

Sommers's (2006) study of mock juries is consistent with these findings of how the presence of racial diversity affected the majority. Sommers had racially diverse (four Whites and two Blacks), and homogeneous (six Whites) mock juries watch and discuss a case involving a Black defendant. At the group level, he found that diverse groups deliberated significantly longer about the case than did homogeneous groups. Notably, he also found that White jurors in racially diverse groups mentioned more novel facts but at the same time expressed fewer errors (or factual inaccuracies) about the case compared to White jurors in racially homogeneous groups.

In another study, Phillips and Loyd (2006) looked at small groups that were homogeneous or diverse with respect to a regional affiliation (North or South campus), deciding which of three companies their company should acquire. Even on a task completely unrelated to the dimension of diversity, they found that the presence of a team member from the other side of campus aided the expression of unique perspectives held by majority group members. Majority group members who had a different perspective than the other two group members about which company should be acquired spoke more and reported feeling that the group was more positive and accepting and feeling more comfortable in a diverse group (i.e., when there was one person present from the other side of campus) than in homogeneous groups.

Given this body of results, we might ask why this happens. There are three likely reasons why diversity in a team or group is able to facilitate information sharing. The first reason is that the presence of diversity increases expectations of different perspectives and complex thinking. As discussed, diverse social categories or surface differences act as a prime or signal to the group that there may be latent opinion differences present in the group. Exposure to different perspectives has been shown to facilitate divergent thinking (Gruenfeld, 1995; Nemeth, 1985). Thus, the presence of diversity in a group and the related expectation of different perspectives likely increase the anticipation of integrating multiple perspectives and divergent thinking.

The other reason is that the presence of diversity reduces concerns about disagreement. Because people expect more disagreement from those who are socially dissimilar from themselves, a disagreement that arises in a diverse group is likely to be more tolerated than disagreement that arises in a homogeneous setting. Phillips (2003) found that individuals expressed more surprise and irritation when a socially similar other disagreed with them than when a dissimilar other disagreed. As a result, the presence of diversity should make the presence of differences more expected, resulting in less surprise and other negative reactions.

Finally, the presence of diversity seems to reduce the conformity pressure that can inhibit people's willingness to actually discuss their different perspectives. Diversity scholars have long lamented that the positive benefits of latent diversity of knowledge and opinions in diverse groups seem to be offset by negative interpersonal friction and tension (Mannix & Neale, 2005). However, recent findings suggest that reduced concerns about relationships and interpersonal harmony in diverse groups actually increase individuals' willingness to engage in discussing disagreement in diverse as opposed to homogeneous settings. In fact, Loyd, Wang, Phillips, and Lount (2013) found that participants expressed fewer "relationship concerns" when they faced disagreement from a dissimilar other than from a similar other. The homogeneous setting with its high expectations of agreement created conformity pressure and concerns about damaging relationships through discussing different perspectives, making it much more difficult for disagreement to get expressed and discussed (Loyd et al., 2013).

If the presence of differences can be so beneficial to groups, why do we see such mixed results in studies looking at the performance of diverse teams (e.g., Harrison & Klein, 2007; Meyer, 2017; van Dijk et al., 2012; van Knippenberg & Schippers, 2007)? To answer that question, we need to look more closely at the categories and the meaning the differences suggest. Much of the literature on diversity focuses on proportional differences between subgroups while treating differences as equivalent. However, work on status characteristics theory (Berger, Cohen, & Zelditch, 1972) demonstrates that we attach status to many categories that affect how we interact with and respond to those who are high versus low status in ways that are important for group performance. I believe that status is one of the mechanisms that can offset the benefit of diversity in groups.

How Status Gets in the Way

Status is the relative value or respect associated with or given to one individual or group relative to another (Magee & Galinsky, 2008). By some accounts, status is a natural part of how we orient ourselves in society, and humans seek hierarchy to explain the world around them and understand their place and role within it (Magee & Galinsky, 2008). Status may be achieved or ascribed. Achieved status characteristics are those that are gained through merit or effort, such as through one's occupation; whereas ascribed status characteristics are those assigned to you by virtue of mostly fixed attributes or ones over which you have little or no control, such as age, race, and sex. Higher achieved status is understandably associated with greater attributions of competence, and higher ascribed status is associated with greater opportunities for persuasion, influence, and higher attributions of competence than lower ascribed status (Berger, Fisek, Norman, & Zelditch, 1977; Carli, 1990; Fiske, 2012; Ridgeway & Berger, 1986). Status is highly associated with many demographic categories, in part because of the stereotypes of incompetence (both generalized and context-specific) associated with them (Fiske, Cuddy, Glick, & Xu, 2002). Further, visible or salient differences between people make it more likely that demographic differences will be attended to and used to explain differences in behavior and performance. Thus, status is an important lens to consider in diverse groups.

With respect to decision making, in diverse groups where people are likely to differ in their social status, some group members will be seen as more competent and worthy of attention than others. As discussed previously, the presence of diversity (or someone who is different) can act as a signal that different perspectives are present in the group, regardless of whether that person's category is low or high status. However, status may moderate whether the presence of that individual also reduces concerns about disagreement and conformity pressure. For different perspectives to reduce conformity pressure, those perspectives must first be seen as valuable and legitimate, and whether the person who possesses (or is expected to have) the different perspective is high or low status can affect those assessments of legitimacy. Recall the famous Asch experiments (Asch, 1951) where participants were shown two lines with different lengths and then asked which line was longer after hearing the erroneous responses of several confederates (i.e., trained actors). In Asch's studies, the group was quite homogeneous with respect to gender, age, and race, and the confederates and participants were all White college-aged men. Thus, we would expect strong conformity pressure under these circumstances. In fact, a surprising number of participants felt so much pressure to conform to the group that they reported the wrong answer to a clearly objective question (Asch, 1951). However, when one of the confederates (a dissenter) was instructed to give the correct answer, it alleviated the conformity pressure on the participants and rates of conformity dropped from 32 percent to less than 5 percent (Asch, 1951).

Imagine, however, a diverse group but one in which the confederate dissenter (the person giving the correct answer) is not only obviously "different" but presumed incompetent. Would their presence still help the participant resist conformity? A replication of the Asch studies introduced the idea that the effect of the confederate giving the correct answer (i.e., the dissenter) might be weaker if the confederate seems less competent by having that individual wear thick-rimmed glasses and implying that he might not see very well, a relevant concern for the visual task (Allen & Levine, 1971). Even this small change affected the rates of conformity. Participants were less likely to resist conforming than previously, suggesting that the confederate's opinion was seen as less valuable.

Imagine, now, a group where the person in the minority is a member of a low-status group and likely seen as incompetent – for example, an ethnic minority or someone physically disabled. In this case, their presence and perspectives may also not be fully valued. This is consistent with some work done by Thomas-Hunt and Phillips (2004) looking at gender and expertise where groups participated in a male-typed survival task. The group expert was a member of the group with the best individual score on the survival task. They found that groups with female experts performed worse on the task than groups with male experts. Further, female experts were perceived as less expert and were less influential than male non-experts. Groups were less able to take advantage of the expertise within them when it was possessed by a female instead of a male expert, presumably because the lower status of women in the male-typed context resulted in their being perceived as less expert than men. Thus, although the presence of diversity can suggest the existence of different perspectives and ease the expression of those perspectives, even from those who are not expected to hold them, status can interrupt this process by reducing the expected and perceived value of some members' contributions.

Tools for Realizing the Full Potential of Diversity

Taking these preceding findings into account, we may ask ourselves what we can do to relieve these effects. I suggest a few tools for individuals and managers (or team leaders) that may increase the extent to which we are able to realize more potential in diverse teams.

First, for individuals, it is problematic for anyone to be identified primarily through the lens of social category membership, but this risk is even higher if that social category conveys low status and, by extension, low competence. Thus, when you provide information about your specific knowledge, information, and experiences, others have an increased ability to see you as a unique individual. Emphasizing these individual characteristics and traits will not necessarily be sufficient to overcome all the obstacles to influencing others; other group members will still need to be motivated to consider these attributes and overcome the tendency to attend to opinion-confirming information. However, at least if the attributes are mentioned, they will have the potential to be accessible and utilized.

Second, as a corollary to the first point of individuating yourself, sell your strengths. Do not leave it to others to recognize your contributions and talents. For members of low-status categories, information that is counter-stereotypical may go even further in reducing reliance on category-based stereotypes. For example, when I tell people that I have bachelor's and master's degrees in civil engineering, something that is not typically associated with

African-American females or many social scientists, it probably helps boost perceptions of my maths competence and perhaps my general competence as well.

Finally, as individuals, it is important for us to accept some level of discomfort when interacting with others, particularly those whom we see as different from ourselves. There has been much debate about the interpersonal tension associated with diverse teams (Mannix & Neale, 2005), and this has been seen as the "down-side" of diversity. However, more recently scholars have suggested and shown that homogeneous teams may suffer from too much cohesion and concern about getting along at the expense of sharing and discussing their divergent viewpoints (Apfelbaum, Phillips, & Richeson, 2014; Loyd et al., 2013). Instead, the reduced concern that everyone must "get along" helps individuals in diverse teams to be more willing to discuss their disagreement with positive benefits for team outcomes. Although diverse environments may be less cohesive than homogeneous ones, they are unlikely to be corrosive. Perhaps if we realize that a little discomfort goes a long way to helping diverse teams to realize their full potential, we will be more willing to accept it.

As managers, a number of steps can be taken to help realize the potential of your team. First, be aware of your "category-based" expectations of others and encourage the members of your team to do the same. Increasing awareness of the biases and stereotypes we have about others can increase motivation to individuate others. One tool to help increase this awareness is the Implicit Association Test. This is a test developed by social psychologists (Project Implicit, n.d.) that allows people to see the unconscious connections in their minds between different categories (e.g., women and men with home and career, or light and dark skin with assessments of good and bad. To learn more about and take the IAT, go to https://implicit.harvard.edu/implicit/).

Second, work on team structure and put effort into creating more diverse teams. Go beyond your standard sources when finding talent for your teams; overinvest in seeking out talent from different sources. Because of our natural tendencies toward homophily, or associating with others who are similar to ourselves, different team members are likely to have different networks. Utilize the networks of all your employees to help diversify your teams.

Finally, managers play a critical role in team formation and development. Diversity in your teams can increase information processing and complexity, but status markers can make you miss out on valuable knowledge. Therefore, managers should not only actively solicit different perspectives; they also should individuate team members by identifying and highlighting the special talents and contributions each member brings to the team (their "expertise"). When differences are expressed, respected, and considered, we can begin to realize more of the potential diversity represents.

Conclusion

Diversity in group settings is beneficial to both the processes and the outcomes. It encourages new thinking and constructive disagreement, fostering new ideas. However, what exactly diversity means and how to achieve diversity in group settings are complicated by the fact that characteristics that define diversity are tied to social status in most cases. We need to be aware of the fact that we are viewed by others through social lenses and that we ourselves also view others through the same lenses.

View from Practice: Engaging Teams for Business Success at PwC
ANNE DONOVAN

Diversity is a hot topic for me. At PwC, I am responsible for culture and thinking about things that are facing us as a business. We deal with diversity every single day: we work in teams, and virtually nothing is done individually. In those teams, we have racial, gender, and generational diversity.

When I started at the firm in 1983, I acted like a man. We women wore suits that matched nylons just because we did not wear pants. It was too wild to wear pants at the time. You did not talk about being a woman. You just went along like all the men went along. Actually, if you were really good, you played golf, or you did things that let you participate with the men. We never talked about race, let alone sexual orientation. We have come a long way since then, even though we are not there, yet.

As a company, PwC's biggest goal is retention. Retention is not just an HR topic. It is a business case. We estimate that it costs us $100,000 every time someone walks out the door. One percent of turnover costs PwC $35 million a year. To facilitate retention, we expect our leaders, our partners, and our managers not only to acknowledge differences but to celebrate them, and to talk about doing so, because only then will you be able to keep that person around. If you cannot be your whole self at PwC, you will not stay, and then we lose you – and money.

At first, we thought we should treat everyone the same. We thought that was the right thing to do as a firm. Then we realized that everyone was not the same. I believe the biggest change in practice is the idea that it is okay to be different. In fact, we want people to be different. We want people to bring diversity to the teams. We want our people to think differently because if everyone in the room looks the same way, we are not going to come to the best decision.

We work with experts and organizations to improve diversity at PwC. For example, we have worked with Dr Banaji, one of the authors of the book called *Blindspot: Hidden Biases of Good People* (Banaji & Greenwald, 2016), on racial diversity. Our work with Dr Banaji helped us to encourage our employees to identify their blind spots and make changes. For gender diversity, we have partnered with the HeForShe Organization (www.heforshe.org) and have done a lot of work. HeForShe organization is a campaign initiated by UN Women in an effort to achieve gender equality. While it would be great for a female to have a mentor who is also a female, it limits the number of mentors you can have. This also puts undue pressure on women, because they have to mentor everyone. Even though many women enjoy mentoring other women, they cannot mentor every woman they meet. Thus, we started asking ourselves, "How do you get a man to be your mentor? And how do we motivate men to mentor women?" We have had our male leaders pledge from a HeForShe perspective to mentor and bring along women in the organization.

Finally, there is generational diversity. Eighty percent of our employees are millennials at PwC. Globally, the average age of 220,000 employees is twenty-nine. We started facing this issue about seven years ago when our partners started coming into our offices in HR and saying, "What is wrong with the people we are hiring?" Managers and supervisors realized that there were fundamental differences between the new generation of employees and the employees from previous generations. We put evidence-based research behind what we saw so that we could make some decisions. Thus, partnered with the University of South Carolina, we conducted a study (PwC, 2013) and discovered some valuable information. People who were born between 1965 and 1979 are called Gen X. These are the leaders of Corporate America now. As a Gen Xer, you are happy at work (a) if you have control over what you are doing, (b) if what you are doing is good developmentally, and (c) if it is interesting and you are getting paid enough. As a firm, this was the lens we were using to make decisions.

By contrast, millennials, those born between 1980 and 1995, care about how it feels. They are all about how it feels. Is it loving? Am I getting support? Am I getting appreciated? Is it flexible? How well does my team work together? This is a major gap in Corporate America, the difference between Gen X and millennials. Millennials want to do everything in teams. They want flexibility, and they want to be loved. I spend my time convincing my own firm, and now I am working with some of our clients to say that millennials are their audience or their market and that we need to cater to what they want. We have made a huge investment in order to address this, using evidence-based research that shows we need to behave differently in order to bring millennials along. It is a business imperative for us, to change the way we behave.

Integrating Research and Practice: Diverse Teams

BETH A. LIVINGSTON

Two lauded experts on diversity in teams combine their knowledge in this section that draws on research-related and practical expertise. First, Dr Denise Lewin Loyd, of the University of Illinois, describes the rich research history surrounding diversity and teams, focusing on how diversity actually functions in teams. Next, Anne Donovan from PricewaterhouseCoopers adds a colorful account of how diversity in teams manifests in the real world of everyday teamwork and coordination. Together, these two essays belie the oft-heard criticism that academic research fails to bridge the research-practice divide to produce useful and practical implications for employers and employees alike. The inspiration from research and practice is plentiful.

Donovan's message complements the research presented by Loyd perfectly, demonstrating that candid communication and information sharing within diverse groups are critical components often overlooked by managers and scholars alike. Loyd's research demonstrating the effect of diversity on majority group members provides the first opportunity for insight. As Donovan noted, making diversity something that men are held accountable for and something that they believe in is key to PwC's success with their diversity and inclusion efforts. While making the business case for diversity may seem simple, PwC's efforts have absolutely been motivated by the inordinate cost of turnover (and the importance of retention). Loyd's research expands the business case beyond the cost of turnover, demonstrating the innovation and critical thinking benefits that can be afforded not just to women and racial minorities, but also to men and to White employees in those workgroups. These unexpected benefits make supporting group diversity a good decision not just to prevent turnover but also to create organizational value.

Likewise, Loyd mentioned the importance of implicit association tests and similar tools to help individual employees become aware of their own "category-based" expectations of others. Donovan's mention of Banaji and Greenwald's *Blind Spot* echoes this research-based recommendation. When you are aware of your own hang-ups regarding gender, race, or other category-based individual differences, you are likely to be more comfortable with the friction that is necessary to create innovation and creativity in solutions and decision making. This is also more likely to bring people from diverse groups together under a broad umbrella of inclusion, as every person has category-based expectations; candidly admitting and discussing them is a way to make diversity something that matters to all employees.

Finally, it is important to recognize the status differences that occur in groups. Sometimes, a focus on "diversity" can purposefully preclude discussion of power and status. Loyd's research specifically indicates that understanding the role of status is critically important to the effectiveness of diverse groups and that overlooking it can reduce the information sharing that occurs to promote innovation and creativity. Donovan's presentation mirrors this – that making both high-level and mid-level managers accountable for diversity makes the role of status central to the conversation. When managers and group leaders are held accountable for the diversity of their groups, and the ways their groups interact, they become more aware of status in the groups they manage. They are also more likely to promote information sharing and create an environment where dissent is both welcomed and valued.

Loyd emphasized the danger of putting people in a box, whether of race or gender. PwC's millennial study may seem to create a "limiting presumption" by generalizing about millennials. PwC's effort to understand millennials needs to be understood as an effort to encourage two different groups of people with different values and attitudes to understand each other better because misunderstanding between Gen Xers and millennials was creating conflicts in the organization. It is always a delicate balancing act between learning about a group as a whole to create a better inclusive climate and acknowledging individuality within that group. Constantly examining one's own biases will help manage them.

Promoting diversity in teams – particularly gender diversity – has become in vogue, partly because it is a reality of the availability of talent and partly because of institutionalized norms of inclusion. However, Loyd's research and Donovan's experience combined show us some of the ways that more value can be extracted from diverse teams – via awareness of bias, communication about diversity and status at all levels of the organization, and accountability for results, including – but also beyond – turnover and retention.

Managerial and Organizational Actions for Creating Inclusive Teams

ELLEN ERNST KOSSEK AND KYUNG-HEE LEE

Managerial Actions

- **Build a safe environment for diverse teams to thrive.**
As a manager, you play a critical role in fostering a safe environment where everyone can contribute and exchange ideas without worrying about being shut down, rejected, or even punished (Bradley, Postlethwaite, Klotz, Hamdani, & Brown, 2012). Research shows that psychological safety is related to increased team creativity

(Lee, Choi, & Kim, 2018) and team performance (Bradley et al., 2012). Harvard professor Amy Edmondson defines psychological safety as "a shared belief held by members of a team that the team is safe for interpersonal risk-taking" (Edmondson, 1999: 354).

Google identified psychological safety as one of the key factors that contribute to successful teams after conducting a two-year study (Rozovsky, 2015). Google's head of industry, Paul Santagata, recommends that managers periodically identify and measure the level of psychological safety in their increasingly diverse teams and take actions to foster psychological safety (Delizonna, 2017). Santagata suggests that one way to foster psychological safety is to *remind team members that, despite differences, we are all human.* Team members should be reminded that everyone shares basic human commonalities, such as having vulnerabilities, hopes, and dreams; desiring respect and happiness; and wanting their opinions and beliefs to be valued (Delizonna, 2017).

Another action that managers can take is to actively seek to develop a culture where members are more likely to hold perceptions that value working in a diverse group. For example, managers can identify, emphasize, and openly recognize the key expertise of each member and the value it brings to the teams. They can also encourage members to see the benefits of sharing diverse views and of not being defensive when engaging in critical reflection (Ellwart, Bundgens, & Rack, 2017). Another team development strategy to foster effective interactions and safety in diverse teams is to make it less likely that team members will be defensive when sharing views. Prior to a difficult conversation where there is likely to be disagreement, the manager may socialize members (1) to prepare how to present their point of view from a third-party perspective so that reactions and questions can be anticipated, and (2) to be curious to try and understand what led to the problem and seek win-win solutions (rather than digging in to one perspective right from the start) when addressing a problem or trying to resolve a team conflict (Delizonna, 2017).

- **Be aware of your own biases and be a role model for how to manage them effectively.**

All individuals have some biases that are difficult to reduce, and managers are no exception. Modeling showing awareness and managing biases can enable managers to help diverse teams flourish, as it will shape equity in managerial decisions on hiring, work assignment, and team member assessment. As a first step, David Rock, the president of the NeuroLeadership Institute, which uses scientific members to advance leadership (Tarallo, 2018), recommends that managers can accept and share with team members that everyone including him or herself has a bias. He also suggests that managers point out that many individuals hold a similarity bias – the belief that "people like me are better than others" – whether it is a similarity of gender, race, or religion. He recommends that in order to use the similarity bias to achieve a positive outcome, managers need to go beyond identity group differences to focus on commonalities among team members such as shared sports interests, family birth order, child status, or common hobbies.

Organizational Actions

- **Educate managers on the benefits of diverse teams, and implement strategies to mitigate hiring biases.**

Although creating effective diverse teams is critical for organizational success, managers may not be aware of the many ways in which diversity and diverse teams can benefit companies. A recent study of venture capital firms reported that a 10 percent increase in female partners hired yielded a 1.5 percent increase in fund return and 9.7 percent more profitable exits (Gompers & Kovvali, 2018). Another study found that having diverse top management teams is related to higher organizational innovation (Talke, Salomo, & Kock, 2011). Sharing such facts with managers will increase managers' awareness of the benefits of diverse teams.

Although hiring diverse employees is the first key step to building diverse teams in organizations, implicit bias often hinders hiring diverse team members. Implicit bias is activated "when negative valence is unconsciously associated with a social object (e.g., women) and the biased behavior is not that obvious" (Kossek, Su, & Wu, 2018: 235). Organizational members often tend to have implicit and explicit assumptions about what qualifications or characteristics constitute successful employees, such as assumptions about education, experience, gender, or race. Based on these assumptions, organizations end up repeatedly hiring people similar to past hires in a biased belief that they are following a formula that leads to success (Mackenzie & Correll, 2018). This leads to what is called homosocial reproduction, the tendency of incumbents to select new members who are similar to themselves (Rivera, 2013). Over time, this leads to team homogeneity instead of diversity.

Since teams increasingly are making hiring decisions, team leaders as well as managers need to be trained on how to avoid implicit biases in hiring that limit the creation of diverse teams. For example, members should be asked to examine prevailing biases that are often associated with success, such as the belief that men are better than women at math. The prevalence of such biases in many societies is one reason why the STEM (science, technology, engineering, and mathematics) field still has many more men than women. One experimental study (Bertrand & Mullainathan, 2004) found that a man's chance of being hired for a job that required math skills was twice as high as a woman's regardless of the gender of the hiring party. When a job requires a certain skill set, organizations need to carefully examine any biases associated with that skill set and educate members involved in hiring decisions.

Another example regarding educational background biases as indicators of success comes from Intuit, a business and financial software company. Despite the fact that their top management team, including their CEO and CFO, did not graduate from Ivy League schools, the firm emphasized recruiting new talent only from top universities. Once they realized the implicit bias in their hiring practices and its ramifications, they examined their hiring criteria closely and made changes to ensure that they were hiring people based more on the skills that the company needed than on where people were educated (Mackenzie & Correll, 2018).

Some experts (Bertrand & Mullainathan, 2004) recommend blinding parts of the hiring process that may elicit implicit biases – such as names of schools on a résumé. Bertrand and Mullainathan's (2004) experimental study found that a résumé with Caucasian Anglo-sounding names received 50 percent more call-backs than the same resume with Black-sounding names in an experimental study. Intuit built on this research and has now started blinding candidates' schools and prior employers during the hiring process (Mackenzie & Correll, 2018). Some companies are using software such as GapJumper that assesses job-relevant skills and reduces implicit biases (Miller, 2016). GapJumper reported that the companies that used their software increased the chances of getting a first-round interview for minority and women candidates by 40 percent (Feldmann, 2018). Although partial blinding in hiring will not be suitable for all situations and will not eliminate all implicit biases, when used effectively, it can help build more diverse teams.

Another strategy to foster diverse teams is to adopt team incentives to hire a diverse team, and socialize members on the importance of having an open mind and selecting team members who are more likely to have personalities that are open to experience and exploring differences (Homan et al., 2008). Studies also recommend designing team tasks to require the need for diversity in task design – such as designing complex teams to have a task that requires integrating diverse components at the same time that the team is designed to be interdependent (Wegge, Roth, Neubach, Schmidt, & Kanfer, 2008).

- **Train managers and teams on how to manage the social interaction and potential conflict challenges of diverse teams.**

While hiring diverse members is a good first step toward building diverse teams, organizations will not experience the benefits of diverse teams unless they help team leaders learn the challenges of managing diverse teams and how to overcome them. One of these challenges is that working in a diverse team is hard (Rock, Grant, & Grey, 2016). Members need to be educated that while research shows that team members tend to feel more comfortable working in a homogeneous team than in a diverse team, for many tasks, diverse teams perform better than homogeneous teams. A study (Phillips, Liljenquist, & Neale, 2008) involving fraternity and sorority members provides a good example. Researchers asked teams consisting of three members from the same fraternity or sorority to solve a murder mystery. The team members were given twenty minutes to discuss the case and come up with an answer. After five minutes, a new member was introduced to the teams. Half of the teams had a new member from their own fraternity or sorority, and the other half had a new member who was not from their own house. After twenty minutes, the homogeneous teams reported smoother processes and had more confidence in their answers than the diverse teams. However, adding a diverse member to the team increased their chance of finding the right suspect from 29 percent to 60 percent.

In order to help managers and team members overcome the likely initial discomfort of working in a diverse team, Stanford University researchers Mackenzie and Correll (2018) have suggested educating team leaders on the concept of "additive contribution," which they define as the skills, experience, and values that a team member brings to the team. Team leaders can design team-oriented assignments that require a contribution from each team member to succeed to help team members appreciate additive contribution. Richard Farnell (2016), an army officer who has experience in training many new recruits, emphasizes the importance of using team-oriented assignments, such as a team obstacle course that requires every member of the team to clear the course together. After the completion of the assignment, the team leader then can emphasize each member's contribution, reinforcing the value of additive contribution and creating a bond at the same time.

Organizations can also train members on how to handle conflicts in diverse teams. Research shows that members may perceive diverse teams as having incompatibility and greater conflict compared to homogeneous teams (Toegel & Barsoux, 2016). As an example, in a series of experimental studies (Phillips, Lount, Sheldon, & Rink, 2016), researchers asked students to assess the level of conflict in a discussion, where the teams were either homogeneous (all White or all Black members) or diverse (a mix of White and Black members). The students consistently reported higher levels of conflict in the diverse team condition, regardless of whether they were provided with a transcript, a video, or an audio of the same discussion. Moreover, when asked whether they would provide more resources for the team, students were less likely to grant the requested resources to the diverse team. Such social experiments suggest that organizations need to be careful in managing inaccurate social dynamics harming perceptions of the performance of diverse teams that may shape unequal assignment of resources.

Organizations can also proactively teach members *how to prevent conflict* in diverse teams, because preventing conflict is easier than resolving conflict. Ginka Toegel and Jean-Louis Barsoux, professors at the International Institute for Management Development (IMD), suggest that team leaders facilitate short thirty-minute conversations based on how people look, act, speak, think, and feel in order to help teams manage diversity (Toegel & Barsoux, 2016). Team leaders need to explain in advance that the purpose of the conversations is to explore areas of possible conflict by sharing and examining one's preferences and expectations. These conversations are most helpful at the beginning of the team formation or when a new member joins the team. In facilitating the conversations, Toegel and

Barsoux suggest that all the questions start with "In your world ..." and all the statements begin with "In my world ..." They argue that this practice helps participants to realize that where our differences or biases come from is less important than the fact that we all have differences and biases.

As an example of an exercise, they recommend encouraging team members to talk about what they first notice about a person and what impression it makes on them. Team members can realize how seemingly innocuous things such as what you wear (khakis or a suit or a sweater) can create bias and distance between members. Another exercise involves conversations that focus on which behaviors are appropriate or inappropriate (e.g., physical touching, hugging, distance) and are valued or discouraged (e.g., punctuality, volunteering, assertiveness) across individuals, genders, and cultures. Understanding one another's values and comfort level will help prevent future misunderstandings. For example, some people are always punctual, but others are always late. The latter may be viewed as disrespectful in some cultures and not a problem in others. Questions about punctuality that elicit statements like "In my world, deadlines are just a suggestion," or "In my world, you always meet the deadline," or "In my world, missing a deadline means you are irresponsible" help team members understand others' expectations and how to manage differences.

Toegel and Barsoux's (2016) exercise regarding conversations on language focuses on what, how, and how much to communicate. Team members can learn how jokes, humor, sarcasm, criticism, or casual suggestions can be considered appropriate. For example, an individual may casually say, "Let's have coffee soon," to a team member without meaning it, but the team member may take it seriously. If this is viewed as not keeping a "promise," a team member may decide that the individual is not to be trusted. Another exercise they recommend for diverse teams is conversations on thinking, which focus on how people think about work, including how they make decisions and solve problems. Some people are good at details while others are good at seeing the big picture. Some people thrive under pressure while others struggle under pressure. Learning different approaches and reactions to different work situations can help team leaders assign team members to tasks where they can perform best and avoid failure, and allow members to value what each person brings to the table.

Another conversational exercise on feelings focuses on how emotions are expressed in teams. Discussing appropriate ways to express negative emotions is important because expressing them too often or inappropriately can do as much harm to the team as bottling them up. For example, statements like "In my world, your voice gets raised when you are passionate about something," and "In my world, a raised voice means conflict and trouble," or "In my world, crying during a meeting is considered unprofessional," and "In my world, crying is a natural response when you are upset" can facilitate discussions on how emotions need to be handled and expressed in a team setting.

REFERENCES

Allen, V.L., & Levine, J.M. (1971). Social support and conformity: The role of independent assessment of reality. *Journal of Experimental Social Psychology*, 7(1), 48–58. https://doi.org/10.1016/0022-1031(71)90054-0.

Allen, V.L., & Wilder, D.A. (1979). Group categorization and attribution of belief similarity. *Small Group Behavior*, 10(1), 73–80. https://doi.org /10.1177/0090552679101006.

Ancona, D.G., & Caldwell, D.F. (1992). Demography and design: Predictors of new product team performance. *Organization Science*, 3(3), 321–41. https://doi.org/10.1287/orsc.3.3.321.

Antonio, A.L., Chang, M.J., Hakuta, K., Kenny, D.A., Levin, S., & Milem, J.F. (2004). Effects of racial diversity on complex thinking in college students. *Psychological Science, 15*(8), 507–10. https://doi.org/10.1111/j.0956-7976.2004.00710.x.

Apfelbaum, E.P., Phillips, K.W., & Richeson, J.A. (2014). Rethinking the baseline in diversity research: Should we be explaining the effects of homogeneity? *Perspectives on Psychological Science, 9*(3), 235–44. https://doi.org/10.1177/1745691614527466.

Asch, S.E. (1951). Effects of group pressure upon the modification and distortion of judgment. In H. Guetzkow (Ed.), *Groups, leadership and men*, 222–36. Pittsburgh, PA: Carnegie Press.

Banaji, M.R., & Greenwald, A.G. (2016). *Blindspot: Hidden biases of good people*. New York: Bantam.

Berger, J., Cohen, B.P., & Zelditch, M. (1972). Status characteristics and social interaction. *American Sociological Review, 37*(3), 241–55. https://doi.org/10.2307/2093465.

Berger, J., Fisek, M.H., Norman, R.Z., & Zelditch, M., Jr. (1977). *Status characteristics and social interaction*. New York: Elsevier.

Bertrand, M., & Mullainathan, S. (2004). Are Emily and Greg more employable than Lakisha and Jamal? A field experiment on labor market discrimination. *The American Economic Review, 94*(4), 991–1013. https://doi.org/10.1257/0002828042002561.

Bradley, B.H., Postlethwaite, B.E., Klotz, A.C., Hamdani, M.R., & Brown, K.G. (2012). Reaping the benefits of task conflict in teams: The critical role of team psychological safety climate. *Journal of Applied Psychology, 97*(1), 151–8. https://doi.org/10.1037/a0024200.

Campbell, K., & Mínguez-Vera, A. (2008). Gender diversity in the boardroom and firm financial performance. *Journal of Business Ethics, 83*(3), 435–51. https://doi.org/10.1007/s10551-007-9630-y.

Carli, L. (1990). Gender, language, and influence. *Journal of Personality and Social Psychology, 59*(5), 941–51. https://doi.org/10.1037/0022-3514.59.5.941.

Chen, F.F., & Kenrick, D.T. (2002). Repulsion or attraction? Group membership and assumed attitude similarity. *Journal of Personality and*

Social Psychology, 83(1), 111–25. https://doi.org/10.1037/0022
-3514.83.1.111.

Cox, T., & Blake, S. (1991). Managing cultural diversity: Implications for
organizational competitiveness. *Academy of Management Executive, 5*(3),
45–56. https://doi.org/10.5465/ame.1991.4274465.

Cox, T.H., Lobel, S.A., & McLeod, P.L. (1991). Effects of ethnic group
cultural differences on cooperative and competitive behavior on a
group task. *Academy of Management Journal, 34*(4), 827–47. https://doi
.org/10.5465/256391.

Delizonna, L. (2017, 24 August). High-performing teams need
psychological safety. Here's how to create it. *Harvard Business Review*.
Retrieved from https://hbr.org/2017/08/high-performing-teams-need
-psychological-safety-heres-how-to-create-it.

Dobbin, F., & Jung, J. (2011). Corporate board gender diversity and stock
performance: The competence gap or institutional investor bias? *North
Carolina Law Review, 89*, 809–38.

Edmondson, A. (1999). Psychological safety and learning behavior in
work teams. *Administrative Science Quarterly, 44*(2), 350–83. https://doi
.org/10.2307/2666999.

Ellwart, T., Bundgens, S., & Rack, O. (2013). Managing knowledge
exchange and identification in age diverse teams. *Journal of Managerial
Psychology, 28*(7/8), 950–72. https://doi.org/10.1108/JMP-06-2013-0181.

Farnell, R. (2016, 18 July). How U.S. Army basic training turns diverse
groups into teams. *Harvard Business Review*. Retrieved from https://
hbr.org/2016/07/how-u-s-army-basic-training-turns-diverse
-groups-into-teams.

Feldmann, J. (2018, 3 April). The benefits and shortcomings of blind hiring
in the recruitment process. *Forbes*. Retrieved from https://www.forbes
.com/sites/forbeshumanresourcescouncil/2018/04/03/the-benefits
-and-shortcomings-of-blind-hiring-in-the-recruitment-process/.

Fiske, S.T. (2012). Managing ambivalent prejudices: Smart-but-cold and
warm-but-dumb stereotypes. *The Annals of the American Academy of*

Political and Social Science, 639(1), 33–48. https://doi.org/10.1177
/0002716211418444.

Fiske, S., Cuddy, A., Glick, P., & Xu, J. (2002). A model of (often mixed)
stereotype content: Competence and warmth respectively follow
from perceived status and competition. *Journal of Personality and Social
Psychology, 82*(6), 878–902. https://doi.org/10.1037/0022-3514.82.6.878.

Gompers, P., & Kovvali, S. (2018, 1 July). The other diversity dividend.
Harvard Business Review. Retrieved from https://hbr.org/2018/07/
the-other-diversity-dividend.

Gruenfeld, D.H. (1995). Status, ideology, and integrative complexity on
the U.S. Supreme Court: Rethinking the politics of political decision
making. *Journal of Personality and Social Psychology, 68*(1), 5–20. https://
doi.org/10.1037//0022-3514.68.1.5.

Harrison, D.A., & Klein, K.J. (2007). What's the difference? Diversity
constructs as separation, variety, or disparity in organizations. *Academy
of Management Review, 32*(4), 1199–228. https://doi.org/10.5465
/amr.2007.26586096.

Herring, C. (2009). Does diversity pay? Race, gender, and the business
case for diversity. *American Sociological Review, 74*(2), 208–24. https://
doi.org/10.1177/000312240907400203.

Homan, A.C., Hollenbeck, J.R., Humphrey, S.E., van Knippenberg, D.,
Ilgen, D.R., & van Kleef, G.A. (2008). Facing differences with an open
mind: Openness to experience, salience of intra-group differences, and
performance of diverse work groups. *Academy of Management Journal,
51*(6), 1204–22. https://doi.org/10.5465/amj.2008.35732995.

Kossek, E.E., Su, R., & Wu, L. (2017). "Opting out" or "pushed out"?
Integrating perspectives on women's career equality for gender
inclusion and interventions. *Journal of Management, 43*(1), 228–54.
https://doi.org/10.1177/0149206316671582.

Lee, H.W., Choi, J.N., & Kim, S. (2018). Does gender diversity help teams
constructively manage status conflict? An evolutionary perspective
of status conflict, team psychological safety, and team creativity.

Organizational Behavior and Human Decision Processes, 144, 187–99.
https://doi.org/10.1016/j.obhdp.2017.09.005.

Levine, S.S., Apfelbaum, E.P., Bernard, M., Bartelt, V.L., Zajac, E.J., & Stark,
D. (2014). Ethnic diversity deflates price bubbles. *Proceedings of the
National Academy of Sciences, 111*(52), 18524–9. https://doi.org/10.1073/
pnas.1407301111.

Loyd, D.L., Wang, C., Phillips, K., & Lount, R. (2013). Social category
diversity promotes premeeting elaboration: The role of relationship
focus. *Organization Science, 24*(3), 757–72. https://doi.org/10.1287
/orsc.1120.0761.

Mackenzie, L., & Correll, S. (2018, 1 October). Two powerful ways
managers can curb implicit biases. *Harvard Business Review.* Retrieved
from https://hbr.org/2018/10/two-powerful-ways-managers
-can-curb-implicit-biases.

Magee, J., & Galinsky, A. (2008). Social hierarchy: The self-reinforcing
nature of power and status. *Academy of Management Annals, 2,* 351–98.
https://doi.org/10.5465/19416520802211628.

Mannix, E., & Neale, M.A. (2005). What differences make a difference?
The promise and reality of diverse teams in organizations. *Psychological
Science in the Public Interest, 6*(2), 31–55. https://doi.org/10.1111
/j.1529-1006.2005.00022.x.

McLeod, P.L., Lobel, S.A., & Cox, T.H. (1996). Ethnic diversity and
creativity in small groups. *Small Group Research, 27*(2), 248–64. https://
doi.org/10.1177/1046496496272003.

Meyer, B. (2017). Team diversity: A review of the literature. In R. Rico
(Ed.), *The Wiley Blackwell handbook of the psychology of teamwork and
collaborative processes,* 151–75. Chichester: Wiley-Blackwell.

Mill, J.S. (1848). *Principles of political economy with some of their applications
to social philosophy.* London: J.W. Parker.

Miller, C.C. (2016, 25 February). Is blind hiring the best hiring? *New York
Times.* Retrieved from https://www.nytimes.com/2016/02/28
/magazine/is-blind-hiring-the-best-hiring.html.

Nemeth, C. (1985). Dissent, group process, and creativity: The contribution of minority influence. *Advances in group processes*, Vol. 2: 57–75. Greenwich, CT: JAI.

Palacios, S. (2011, 16 September). Multicultural is the wave of the future. *Advertising Age*. Retrieved from https://adage.com/article/the-big -tent/multicultural...wave-future/229842.

Phillips, K.W. (2003). The effects of categorically based expectations on minority influence: The importance of congruence. *Personality and Social Psychology Bulletin*, 29(1), 3–13. https://doi.org/10.1177 /0146167202238367.

Phillips, K.W., Liljenquist, K.A., & Neale, M.A. (2009). Is the pain worth the gain? The advantages and liabilities of agreeing with socially distinct newcomers. *Personality and Social Psychology Bulletin*, 35(3), 336–50. https://doi.org/10.1177/0146167208328062.

Phillips, K.W., Lount, R.B., Sheldon, O., & Rink, F. (2016, 22 February). The biases that punish racially diverse teams. *Harvard Business Review*. Retrieved from https://hbr.org/2016/02/the-biases-that-punish -racially-diverse-teams.

Phillips, K.W., & Loyd, D.L. (2006). When surface and deep-level diversity collide: The effects on dissenting group members. *Organizational Behavior and Human Decision Processes*, 99(2), 143–60. https://doi .org/10.1016/j.obhdp.2005.12.001.

Project Implicit. (n.d.). http://implicit.harvard.edu/implicit/.

PwC. (2013). PwC's NextGen: A global generational study. Retrieved from https://www.pwc.com/gx/en/hr-management-services/pdf/pwc -nextgen-study-2013.pdf.

Ridgeway, C.L., & Berger, J. (1986). Expectations, legitimation, and dominance behavior in task groups. *American Sociological Review*, 51(5), 603–7. https://doi.org/10.2307/2095487.

Rivera, L.A. (2013). Homosocial reproduction. In V. Smith (Ed.), *Sociology of work: An encyclopedia*, 377–80. Thousand Oaks, CA: Sage Publications.

Rock, D., Grant, H., & Grey, J. (2016, 22 September). Diverse teams feel less comfortable – and that's why they perform better. *Harvard Business*

Review. Retrieved from https://hbr.org/2016/09/diverse-teams
-feel-less-comfortable-and-thats-why-they-perform-better.

Rozovsky, J. (2015, 17 November). The five keys to a successful Google
team. *re:Work*. Retrieved from https://rework.withgoogle.com/blog
/five-keys-to-a-successful-google-team/.

Sommers, S.R. (2006). On racial diversity and group decision making:
Identifying multiple effects of racial composition on jury deliberations.
Journal of Personality and Social Psychology, 90(4), 597–612. https://doi
.org/10.1037/0022-3514.90.4.597.

Talke, K., Salomo, S., & Kock, A. (2011). Top management team diversity
and strategic innovation orientation: The relationship and consequences
for innovativeness and performance. *Journal of Product Innovation
Management, 28*(6), 819–32. https://doi.org/10.1111/j.1540-5885
.2011.00851.x.

Tarallo, M. (2018, 21 December). How managers can overcome their personal
biases. Retrieved from https://www.shrm.org/resourcesandtools
/hr-topics/organizational-and-employee-development/pages/self
-aware-managers.aspx.

Thomas-Hunt, M.C., & Phillips, K.W. (2004). When what you know is not
enough: Expertise and gender dynamics in task groups. *Personality and
Social Psychology Bulletin, 30*(12), 1585–98. https://doi.org/10.1177
/0146167204271186.

Toegel, G., & Barsoux, J.-L. (2016, 1 June). How to preempt team conflict.
Harvard Business Review. Retrieved from https://hbr.org/2016/06
/how-to-preempt-team-conflict.

van Dijk, H., van Engen, M.L., & van Knippenberg, D. (2012). Defying
conventional wisdom: A meta-analytical examination of the differences
between demographic and job-related diversity relationships with
performance. *Organizational Behavior and Human Decision Processes,
119*(1), 38–53. https://doi.org/10.1016/j.obhdp.2012.06.003.

van Knippenberg, D., & Schippers, M.C. (2007). Work group diversity.
Annual Review of Psychology, 58, 515–41. https://doi.org/10.1146
/annurev.psych.58.110405.085546.

Wegge, J., Roth, C., Neubach, B., Schmidt, K.-H., & Kanfer, R. (2008). Age and gender diversity as determinants of performance and health in a public organization: The role of task complexity and group size. *Journal of Applied Psychology, 93*(6), 1301–13. https://doi.org/10.1037/a0012680.

Woolley, A.W., Chabris, C.F., Pentland, A., Hashmi, N., & Malone, T.W. (2010). Evidence for a collective intelligence factor in the performance of human groups. *Science, 330*(6004), 686–8. https://doi.org/10.1126/science.1193147.

PART TWO

Gender Inclusion in Industry and Organizational Contexts

5

LEARNING FROM STEM (SCIENCE, TECHNOLOGY, ENGINEERING, MATHS) CONTEXTS

I was taught that the way of progress was neither swift nor easy.

– Marie Curie (1923)

What the Research Tells Us: That None Shall Perish

KELLY MACK, CHRISTIE SAHLEY, AND ORLANDO TAYLOR

With respect to the number of STEM women of color in academic leadership, one thing remains true – more women of color are needed in the academy. Currently, STEM women faculty make up 58 percent and 46 percent of the scientists and engineers in two- and four-year institutions, respectively (National Science Foundation, 2015). Although these percentages reflect a dramatic increase over the 30 percent level of representation of women reported for 2006 (Burrelli, 2008), a closer examination of the status of women science and engineering faculty at four-year colleges and universities reveals that women of color make up only 4.5 percent, 3.7 percent, and 1.2 percent of assistant, associate, and full professors in academic science and engineering disciplines, respectively (National Science Foundation, 2015).

The quality of life for women of color has been examined for more than a century, beginning as early as 1851 with the impromptu speech of Sojourner Truth, a former slave who eloquently articulated the differential treatment of White women as compared to Black women in her speech (Truth, 1851), "Ain't I a Woman?" Since that time, others have sought to explore the status of women of color in the context of the academic STEM disciplines (Ong, Wright, Espinosa, & Orfield, 2010). Arguably, one of the most noted efforts at achieving this was the 1975 meeting of STEM women of color at the American Association for the Advancement of Science. This meeting was unique in that it was the first federally funded initiative that brought together women scientists of color to articulate the "cost" of becoming and thriving in STEM at the intersection of race and gender. One significant outcome of this meeting was a blueprint for change, the *Double Bind Report* (Malcom, Hall, & Brown, 1976), which differentially identified both the culturally intrinsic and societally extrinsic forces that challenge the professional livelihood of women of color in the academic STEM disciplines. Such cultural complexities as the strong traditional gender roles that are highly characteristic of minority communities, the need for same-race/same-gender role models, stereotyping, lack of cultural sensitivity in workplace flexibility considerations, and the disproportionate burden of adverse health conditions and outcomes (Mendoza & Johnson, 2000; Goulden, Frasch, & Mason, 2009; Mack, Rankins, & Winston, 2011) have been justly identified as factors that limit the full participation of women of color in the academic STEM disciplines.

While the fact that none of these challenges can be ascribed to any deficiency in aptitude or fortitude on the part of women of color may occasion a call to action that is grounded in social justice, increasing the number of women of color in the academic STEM disciplines is identified as more than merely "the right thing to do" (Cantor, Mack, McDermott, & Taylor, 2014). Rather, the race-gender intersectional lens through which women of color ask more probing questions and demand direct answers (Laurent-Ottomane, 2012) leads to the levels of excellence in our scientific understanding and predictive models that are needed for pre-eminence in technology, sustainability, health, and engineering. Similarly, in their re-examination of the *Double Bind Report*, Malcom and Malcom (2011) noted that,

> Now it is less about rights versus wrongs and more about support versus neglect; less about the behavior of individuals and a culture that was accepting of bias as the "natural order of things," and more about the responsibilities and action (or inaction) of institutions.

A New Paradigm for Leadership Development

Aside from the scientific advances that result from more inclusivity of women of color in the STEM fields, there is also a vital role that women of color play in leadership. As Laurent-Ottomane (2012) has noted, women of color on corporate boards provide an added dimension that broadens discussions and supports effective problem solving. Sanchez-Hucles and Davis (2010) argue that it is the multiple and intersecting identities of gender and race that interact to produce a distinctly different outcome as a result of the presence of leaders who are women of color.

However, while the percentage of women presidents overall increased between 1986 and 2006 (Caton, 2007), collectively, women of color still make up less than 20 percent of all women college presidents (see table 5.1).

The paucity of STEM women of color in academic leadership, coupled with a steady increase in the average age of college presidents, is predicted to result in a national shortage of leaders who are equipped to meet the evolving demands of higher education (Sanchez-Hucles & Davis, 2010). Such demands require strategic problem-solving skills to simultaneously reform current models of teaching and learning to suit *all* students, including those historically underrepresented in STEM disciplines; negotiate fiscal constraints

Table 5.1. Racial/Ethnic Distribution of Women College Presidents, 1986–2006

	White	African American	American Indian	Hispanic
1986	89%	4%	1%	5%
2006	81%	7%	1.3%	7%

Source: Caton, 2007

while cultivating new faculty reward systems; address shifting racial/ethnic higher-education demographics; provide positive learning environments for all students; and meet contemporary STEM workforce demands. Additionally, these demands call for organizations to design and implement the kind of leadership development that recognizes, fully considers, and manages the lived experiences of those at the intersection of multiple identities.

Indeed, effective leadership development is often seen as an important strategy for addressing the underrepresentation of women of color in academic leadership at all levels, from the department chair through deanships, provostships, and even the presidency. However, most of the existing leadership development interventions have been directed toward "fixing" women of color through individual skills development in negotiation, strategic finance, and budgeting, or through mentoring (Taylor & Mack, 2015). The Women in Engineering Proactive Network (WEPAN), through its framework for creating gender-inclusive organizations, posits that this kind of effort constitutes only a basic level of intervention and fails to achieve the kind of cultural shifts that can bring about lasting and systemic change in the inclusion of marginalized groups. Indeed, a quick review of the most popular leadership development programs for women in the United States reveals that there is a dearth of effort directed toward empowering women of color in STEM for leadership (Taylor & Mack, 2015).

In fact, there is only one known federally funded, graduate, credit-bearing academic-leadership program that is authentically grounded in the lived experience of women of color, and singularly focused on the STEM disciplines. The NSF-funded Opportunities for Underrepresented Scholars (OURS) Program is an established Academic Leadership Certificate Program that is holistically grounded in the inherent assets and attributes of women of color as leaders. The program not only equips individuals for leadership but also strategically addresses the underlying systemic institutional factors that contribute to gender and racial/ethnic disparities in academic leadership. More specifically, through an asset-based model of professional development, participants in this program are empowered to become lifelong learners of higher education theory, policy, and practice, as opposed to mere strategists navigating the complexities of higher education. As such, participants are provided with an understanding that their differentially negative experiences in higher education have less to do with themselves as STEM academicians and more to do with the systemic institutional and socio-political influences that have created and continue to contribute to their marginalization from leadership positions.

OURS is grounded in the Entropic Career Identity Development model (Mack, Rankins, & Woodson, 2013), a conceptual model that uses an action-learning approach to integrate professional education and the lived experiences of STEM women of color with authentic leadership experiences to empower them to respond effectively to the pedagogical and academic leadership challenges of the twenty-first century. In the first three years since its founding, the OURS program has seen marked success – with close to 40 percent of its first cohort of participants ascending to various leadership levels ranging from dean to provost.

Conclusion

It is widely acknowledged that differences among individuals – particularly those derived from the backgrounds, cultures, experiences, and perspectives of underrepresented groups – lead to new and better approaches in discovery and innovation (Page, 2007). This truth is particularly germane to STEM higher education, given its role in developing the nation's next generation of discoverers and innovators. As the potential pool of undergraduate STEM talent continues to diversify, the need for more diverse leadership will only increase and intensify. Women of color, because of their lived experience at the intersection of race *and* gender, provide added dimensions to academic leadership that are key to ensuring the nation's pre-eminence in science and technology. Our goal, then, is to prepare not only this cadre of leaders but also our institutions of higher education – and, indeed, our society – for such leadership.

In the 1975 *Double Bind Report*, Malcom, Hall, and Brown (1976) noted that more efforts toward generating and sustaining a communications network would be necessary for achieving equitable participation of women of color in STEM. To that end, a broad range of ally organizations, industries, and individuals have emerged alongside the OURS Program to accelerate the retention of women of colour in both the STEM disciplines in general and leadership positions more specifically. Such organizations as Black Women in Computing and the Society of STEM Women of Color, Inc., collectively, share a responsibility to ensure that our nation's science and engineering enterprise is as diverse as its population. These organizations also serve to provide overall conceptualization, analysis, and interpretation of data that authentically capture the narratives and worldviews of women of color, which are so sorely needed for achieving excellence in discovery and innovation. Without such national support structures and their contributions to the development of STEM leaders, it is likely that future leadership development programs will continue to be devoid of the influence of the culturally responsive components needed to make them effective. And our institutions, along with the students they serve, will be robbed of the richness of all that twenty-first-century higher education can and *should* offer.

View from Practice: Learning from Successful Women in the STEM Field

MARIANA MONTEIRO

Working for General Electric (GE), I am a part of an environment that promotes creative inclusiveness – one that makes sure that we have equal opportunities. We pursue not only compliance with the rules but also truly diverse perspectives because this is not just a convenient thing that looks good: we believe that it is what drives innovation.

At GE, we are proud to be one of the most innovative companies in the world, a reputation that is due in part to diversity of thought. In this essay, I focus on two topics. First, I discuss the importance of women leaders at the top who can stand up for women's rights and "be the change." Second, I present my observations of successful women in the STEM field.

To make changes in organizations, we need more women leaders at the top, and we need them to actively take part in subverting the status quo. Traditionally, we have adjusted our message to the audience, and the audience has tended to be primarily white males, who have owned and managed the systems. Luckily, that is changing over time: a more diversified portfolio of talent is increasingly present in positions of power and, more importantly, there is a new expectation about freedom and self-directing our lives.

However, there is also a strong tendency – many times not even noticed – still to embrace and not challenge the stereotypes that hinder our progress. Some of us may interpret reality as a zero-sum game: "If you excel professionally, you may not be a great caretaker"; "Because I am very good at listening, there is no need to interject my ideas all the time"; or "The demands of an upper management job are not compatible with personal life."

What concerns me most is that sometimes this is an unconscious process where women know what they want to revolt against but stay in the shallow surface without asserting themselves. We get it "intellectually." We are experts on what should be done, but many do not "actualize" the vision. We park in the potential. A few may break through the self-imposed restrictions and, sure enough, may suffer from impostor syndrome.

We may have learned to be silent about and compliant with the expectations of the mainstream in order to be accepted. This resembles the story of the elephant raised in captivity with a chain on its leg. While young, the elephant tried and tried to move around beyond the reach of the chain, but to no avail. It tried and tried to get the chain off its leg – in vain. The elephant grew up, and finally, his chain was off. However, he did not walk out of his previous circle of movement. He stayed in the familiar circle because he had learned to be helpless. I believe the same thing has happened to many of us. I think it is time to wake up and go out of our own comfort zone. We need to realize that we no longer have the chain. To me, the most interesting part of the concept of learned helplessness is the "learned" part. If the helplessness is learned – in most cases through the socialization process – we can unlearn it. That is how I think institutions, professors, and role models can make a difference. We need to think about some of the patterns and expectations that we have learned that we are blindly complying with, and we need to start to unlearn them and take risk. I want people to look at themselves in the mirror and ask, "Are you complying consciously or unconsciously with that stereotype?" "Can you honestly say you are stretching beyond your comfort zone or are you just playing it safe?" It can truly open your mind. We need to be honest with ourselves and understand that change is possible. Most importantly, we can inspire others to follow through, and this is perhaps where the key resides.

Many women have challenged learned expectations and biases and become successful. When I look around, I see I am surrounded by superb, successful women. One of our strongest employee resources groups at GE is the Women Network. The Women Network with Krannert Executive Education at Purdue University is creating a program, Global Supply Chain, to accelerate even more talent in traditionally male-dominated areas.

Through my career in human resources, I have the privilege of witnessing and learning from great leaders in action, and I can share a few observations. What I have noticed about successful women is that, instead of caving in and singing the same song, they have "effective" voice. They understand the language that is spoken in their business, department, or area. This is correlated with another important aspect, expertise in their field and system knowledge. For example, in business, you need to be versed in financials, market insights, global risk, and connective points between your field and others, regardless of your "specific" area. If you do not know and use the language that is spoken in the circles of decision making, you will be inevitably out of the loop.

In addition to being an expert in the field and, most importantly, being resourceful, successful women state their opinion and are not afraid to admit that there is something they do not know. This is where being resourceful makes a huge difference. Success is aligned with delivering results.

Finally, and this seems to be the trademark of successful colleagues, they advocate for others as well as themselves. I noticed that many women shy away from talking about themselves. Many women reject the idea of self-promotion but embrace the idea of promoting others. However, self-promotion is important to a woman's own success and is a skill that women need to develop. Once you are successful, you have more power to advocate for and sponsor others. Successful women put themselves on the line, and they help other women.

There is still a lot to be done, but the conditions are favorable. We need to start asking ourselves two questions: "Am I hindering my own success by playing it safe and not being bold (and perhaps failing)?" and "How many women have I helped so far?" Spark that chain reaction – we can make a difference for all.

Integrating Research and Practice: STEM Contexts
DIANA BILIMORIA

The importance of the full participation of women in the STEM workforce for U.S. global competitiveness has been well documented (e.g., National Academies, 2007a, 2007b; U.S. Department of Labor, 2007). Yet, even as women are increasingly holders of doctoral degrees in STEM fields, the proportion of women faculty in STEM disciplines in the nation's colleges and universities has been slow to increase, particularly with low participation at the highest levels of the academic hierarchy. Across academic STEM fields, women are less likely than men to be found in full professor positions and are more likely to be assistant professors (National Science Foundation, 2015; Rankins, Rankins, & Inniss, 2014). Fewer differences in rank exist between male and female faculty in early career stages in STEM, but greater differences tend to appear between fifteen and twenty years after receipt of the doctorate. Research also indicates that women are underrepresented in administrative and faculty leadership positions such as presidents, chancellors, provosts, deans, and department chairs (Hollenshead, 2007; Taylor & Mack, 2015). The underrepresentation in college and university administrative leadership is most acute for women of color (Taylor & Mack, 2015) and remains a persistent problem across all ranks within academic STEM disciplines (Mack, Taylor, Cantor, & McDermott, 2014).

Related to the lack of a critical mass of women STEM faculty and few women at the top of the academic hierarchy are resource inequities, barriers, and problems related to differential treatment and evaluation at every level. A groundbreaking study documented that women STEM faculty face micro-aggressions and implicit biases that result in their marginalization and exclusion as faculty colleagues, including their inadvertent receipt of lower salaries, less laboratory space and other resources, exclusion from formal and informal social and professional gatherings, and exclusion from research and teaching collaborations (Massachusetts Institute of Technology, 1999). Rosser (2004) reported that low numbers of women STEM faculty mean that women faculty feel isolated, have limited access to role models and mentors, and have to work harder to gain credibility and respect from their male colleagues (see also Fox, 2010). With constrained access to key academic networks, women junior faculty are left on their own to learn how to navigate the promotion and tenure process in a male-dominated environment. Many women opt out of academic STEM, choosing private-sector positions because they become discouraged by their academic settings (Valian, 2004).

The experiences of women faculty in STEM seem to derive from particular sets of beliefs held about the ideal academic worker (Bailyn, 2003; Benschop & Brouns, 2003; Dean & Fleckenstein, 2007) as someone who "gives total priority to work and has no outside interests or responsibilities" (Bailyn, 2003: 139). Such a mindset contributes directly and indirectly to the treatment and evaluation of women faculty. Silver and colleagues (2006) summarized several aspects that retarded the achievement of full professional equality for women STEM faculty, including demeaning and insulting statements and remarks about women faculty made by the dean and faculty members, "window-dressing" efforts by the dean to support women in engineering programs rather than providing adequate funding for such efforts, public treatment of women faculty in a less respectful manner than male faculty, and comments made to women faculty on the perceived appropriateness of their clothing (Silver et al., 2006).

Institutional Transformation

To address systematic gender inequality in academic STEM – that is, the overt, subtle, or hidden disparities in workforce opportunities and treatment between women and men faculty – and encourage the gender-equity transformation of higher education, the National

Science Foundation (NSF) has established the ADVANCE awards to increase the participation and advancement of women in STEM faculty careers and address structural impediments to women faculty's success in academic STEM (see http://nsf.gov/advance). To date, more than 150 institutions of higher education and associations have benefited from funding from NSF's ADVANCE program, which has become an increasingly widespread and influential national resource for the systemic gender-equity–related transformation of academic STEM across U.S. higher education.

As described in Bilimoria and Liang (2012), gender-equity initiatives undertaken by ADVANCE institutions include pipeline initiatives – initiatives to systematically improve the career trajectories of women and underrepresented minority (URM) faculty at every stage of the academic pipeline – as well as cultural initiatives to improve extant institutional policies, practices, and climate (Bilimoria & Liang, 2012). Pipeline initiatives to address improvements in the individual career trajectories of women and URM faculty at ADVANCE institutions include the following: (a) initiatives to increase the inflow of women into the pipeline (e.g., mentoring programs and workshops targeting graduate and postdoctoral STEM students); (b) initiatives to better equip women to successfully progress in the academic pipeline (e.g., small funding opportunities for research and professional development); and (c) initiatives to improve the institutional structures and processes related to key academic career transition points in the pipeline (e.g., training search committees on unconscious biases and effective recruitment practices). Initiatives to improve institutional policies, practices, and climate include (a) efforts to improve micro (departmental) climates such as by leadership development training of department heads; (b) efforts to improve macro (university) climate, for example by engaging in faculty climate surveys; (c) institutional policy modifications, especially around family-friendly work policies; and (d) research and evaluation efforts to make the institution more equitable, such as salary-equity studies.

Through these targeted initiatives, ADVANCE institutions have been successful in bringing about increased participation and advancement of women STEM faculty. Results reported in Bilimoria and Liang (2012) showed significant improvements across nineteen ADVANCE universities in the workforce participation of women faculty overall and at the assistant and full professor ranks, in leadership, and across the three science and engineering disciplines studied (natural sciences, engineering, and social and behavioral sciences). These universities systematically reduced resource inequities and barriers to recruitment and advancement, transforming their cultures to become more diverse, equitable, and inclusive by implementing a portfolio of simultaneous, varied, and multilevel change practices related to gender equity.

Research to Corporate Practice Implications

Corporations generally lead in the development and implementation of change initiatives. Yet, the example of the ADVANCE institutions is an exception, with higher-education institutions showing how gender diversity, equity, and inclusion can be advanced through the implementation of the ADVANCE institutional transformation model of organization development. As Bilimoria and Liang (2012: 206) put it,

> Simplistic, ad hoc or piecemeal solutions cannot eradicate systematic, historical and widespread gender underrepresentation and inequities ... To overcome existing barriers and inertia, a wider and deeper change is needed. This requires greater reflexivity about everyday gender practices coupled with systematic actions to transform organizational structures, processes, work practices, mental models, and workplace cultures – to enable equal employment, opportunities, treatment, evaluation, and valuing of women and men so that *all* employees can fully

participate, contribute, and develop in their careers and enable their organizations to achieve their goals of effectiveness.

The ADVANCE model indicates that an organization-wide transformational process must be employed to produce lasting gender-equity change. As with other transformational efforts in organizations (e.g., total quality management, process improvements, lean manufacturing, six sigma manufacturing, safety improvements, customer service improvements), gender-equity improvements must also involve high-priority, well-supported, and simultaneous top-down and bottom-up efforts to change the organization's systems, processes, practices, and culture. The success of such a transformational process depends not only on improving diversity, equity, and inclusion within a finite period but also on effectively sustaining and leveraging the results into the future by embedding the changes into the social-cultural fabric of the organization. The example of the NSF ADVANCE initiative in U.S. colleges and universities has shown that such efforts can be successful in transforming organizations to become more gender diverse, equitable, and inclusive.

Managerial and Organizational Actions to Transform STEM Contexts

ELLEN ERNST KOSSEK AND KYUNG-HEE LEE

Managerial Actions

- **Manage gender bias in selection and performance evaluations assessing technical and personal competencies.**

How implicit gender bias may creep into a performance review is a growing problem in the evaluation of technical and personal skills generally, but particularly in STEM fields. When managers increase awareness of and better learn how to manage implicit bias during the performance review, they are more likely to be able to attract and retain STEM female employees. Dr Shelley Correll's research (Correll, 2017) notes a number of ways that gender bias can influence performance and competency assessment. Her analysis suggests that women are often evaluated against a *higher bar* than men. Many studies across different fields repeatedly find that men are evaluated more favorably than women during hiring and performance review processes. As one study of university hiring practices of faculty found, a candidate with a male name was more often selected to be hired than a candidate with a female name, even with the same vita (Steinpreis, Anders, & Ritzke, 1999). Further, women are consistently evaluated as less competent in teaching (MacNell, Driscoll, & Hunt, 2015), customer service (Snipes, Thomson, & Oswald, 2006), and judicial fields (Durham, 2000).

Women often go through *more scrutiny* when being evaluated than men. When presented with the same qualifications and experience, evaluators are more likely to require women to provide more evidence to prove their qualifications and experience (Correll, 2017). Moreover, evaluation criteria can sometimes shift based on employee gender. When men and women are evaluated together, whichever qualifications or experience favor men typically are considered more important. Evidence from an experimental study (Uhlmann & Cohen, 2005) bears this trend out. Participants were asked to rate a male and female candidate for a police chief position. When the male candidate was presented as having more education but less police experience than the female candidate, the raters preferred the male candidate, citing the importance of the education. When the male candidate was presented as having less education but more police experience than the female candidate, the raters still preferred the male candidate, focusing on the experience.

Women also have to overcome a *double bind* (Correll, 2017): a trade-off between being "assertive" and being "likeable" as a challenge in performance assessment that managers should address. Research shows that being assertive tends to be associated with competence in job performance. Yet, while men can be assertive and still be viewed as competent and likeable, evidence shows that assertive women are viewed as not likeable (Rudman, Moss-Racusin, Phelan, & Nauts, 2012). Successful female managers in male-dominant fields such as STEM are less liked and less preferred as bosses than male managers by their employees (Heilman, Wallen, Fuchs, & Tamkins, 2004).

A research team at the Stanford VMware Women's Leadership Lab (Mackenzie, Wehner, & Correll, 2019) argues that the "open box" format of performance evaluation, where managers are given great latitude to describe employees' performance, leaves room for gender bias to creep in. They suggest creating clear evaluation criteria and identifying several measurable outcomes for each employee upfront to be used consistently across gender (Mackenzie et al., 2019). In the experimental study of police chief candidates noted above (Uhlmann & Cohen, 2005), the gender bias disappeared if the raters agreed to commit to determining the competency criteria prior to starting the selection or performance assessment. The Stanford researchers (Mackenzie et al., 2019) also recommend that managers constantly check evaluations against the criteria to see if they find any pattern that may indicate the creeping in of gender bias.

- **Learn how to be a family/life supportive supervisor and combat overwork cultures in STEM contexts.**

Managers can help retain women employees in many fields, including STEM, by learning how to better support employees' family and personal needs. Employees have many non-work roles (e.g., parent, daughter, son, partner, pet owner, volunteer) besides their work role. The needs from these multiple roles often create conflicts, as family/life roles have a tremendous impact, especially on women's careers, because of childbearing and working parents' gendered norms for the domestic division of labor. Although employers have been slow to adapt to employees' growing work-family needs over their lives, 80 percent of workers rated work-life balance as the most essential aspect of an ideal job (Zukin & Szeltner, 2012). Half (51 percent) of workers report that they would change jobs for one with a flextime arrangement (Gallup, 2017). Employee turnover can cost organizations up to 213 percent of a high-skilled employee's salary to train, replace, and recover lost productivity (Bersin, 2013). For example, the employer replacement cost would be $213,000 for an employee making $100,000. That is why Deloitte's work-life initiatives have saved the firm more than $100 million by reducing employee turnover (Transforming Women's Leadership, 2016).

Work-life issues and overwork are particularly problematic for women scientists who are in early career stages and trying to advance their careers in STEM contexts. An NSF-funded study of geoscience faculty conducted by Archie, Kogan, and Laursen (n.d.) found that the competing demands of working long hours, completing graduate or postdoctoral education, earning tenure, and finding a partner and having children all collide for many women in STEM. The authors found that work-life balance is a key contributing factor prompting women with young children to leave tenure-track career paths or STEM careers altogether. Many STEM departments have been found to have "chilly climates" that not only do not respect women's work-life demands but also are unsupportive environments for other forms of career support on the job (Bilimoria & Liang, 2012). For example, despite their qualifications, women may not be considered as a source of leadership talent or for key positions, in part because of implicitly biased concerns over their ability to juggle motherhood and dual-career demands with leadership roles. Research on work-life conflicts and stress has also shown that supervisors who directly interact with employees have the ability to increase or reduce employees' work-life stress (Hammer, Kossek, Anger, Bodner, & Zimmerman, 2011; Kossek, Pichler, Bodner, & Hammer, 2011). Managers' support of employees' work-family/life needs is critical because most work-life practices are informally determined by direct supervisors. Researchers (Hammer, Kossek, Bodner, & Crain, 2013; Kossek & Hammer, 2008) identified four types of supervisors' family/life supportive behaviors that have scientific evidence of health (e.g., sleep, physical health) and well-being benefits for employees, and particularly employees (often women) reporting higher family and non-work stress. These behaviors – developed by professors Leslie Hammer of Portland State and Oregon Health Science Universities, Ellen Ernst Kossek of Purdue University, and their colleagues – include emotional support, instrumental support, role modeling, and creative work-life management.

Emotionally supportive behaviors are defined as supervisor actions that result in employees' perceiving that they are being cared for personally and their non-work needs are supported. An example of emotionally supportive supervisor behavior includes the ability to communicate genuine concerns about employees' work-life challenges, such as recognizing that some employees may need to take personal calls or texts from a family member while at work. Others may need support in separating from work and prefer not to respond to work emails during their personal time. Instrumental supportive behaviors help employees perceive that their managers are willing to help them solve job and personal problems so that they can meet work, personal life, and family demands. Examples include providing employees with more control to manage work schedules, workloads, or other work arrangements as much as possible based on the organization's HR policies. It can also include encouraging team members to help each other in busy peak times, and being apprised of employees' availability as their needs and responsibilities change.

Role-modeling behaviors include managers' actions demonstrating to employees how managers are taking care of their own work-life challenges. Illustrative behaviors include discussing taking time off to attend children's school activities; taking time off from work during the day or leaving early to exercise or volunteer; leaving work at a reasonable hour to show that the organizational culture values having a life outside of work; and modeling that the idea of taking time off for vacations, holidays, or important life events is normal.

The final behavior is demonstrating creative work-family/life management, which is defined as designing work to help employees meet both family/personal needs and work demands. Examples include promoting cross-training and back-up systems for job and staffing coverage; implementing new ways of working together that better support team members' family or personal priorities; and understanding the organization's work-life programs and encouraging employees' use of these resources.

Kossek, Hammer, and their colleagues from the Work Family and Health Network have published a series of studies showing that employees with family demands who had trained supervisors reported improvements in work-family conflict, stress, psychological distress, and depressive symptoms. They also reported greater ability to take family members to the doctor when sick. Training managers in family supportive behaviors across many contexts including health care and IT also resulted in retention and productivity benefits, such as higher performance, lower turnover intentions, higher safety compliance, and increased job satisfaction (Bray et al., 2017; Crain et al., 2014; Hammer et al., 2011; Hammer et al., 2015; Kelly et al., 2014; Kossek et al., 2018; Kossek & Hammer, 2008; Kossek, Hammer, Kelly, & Moen, 2014).

Organizational Actions

- **Challenge high-masculinity cultural values and behaviors that do not support gender inclusion in STEM contexts.**

Forty percent of women with engineering degrees quit or never enter the field to work (Silbey, 2016), and one of the main reasons for women to leave STEM fields is the prevalence of masculinity cultures in STEM organizations (Cheryan, Ziegler, Montoya, & Jiang, 2017) where competition is endorsed, and masculine traits – such as being competitive and aggressive – are valued. After surveying thousands of employees, Drs Berdahl, Glick, and Cooper (2018) identified four masculinity cultural norms. The first norm is showing no weakness, which involves displaying extreme confidence while suppressing any doubt or emotions. The second norm is demonstrating that they are physically strong and can endure working long hours in order to succeed in a masculinity culture. The third norm Berdahl and colleagues identified is that employees are willing to put work first above everything. Taking time off frequently for vacations or family reasons is not valued. The fourth norm is that competition is highly encouraged because the winner takes all, which often undermines trust among employees.

STEM fields are often more vulnerable to having a high-masculinity culture than other fields because masculinity is most prevalent in male-dominated fields (Ely & Kimmel, 2018). It is generally more difficult for women to succeed in organizations with higher masculinity cultures because of the double-bind issue, described earlier in this chapter. To survive the competition, women often have to display masculine traits. However, when women assert masculine traits that are valued for successful men, women tend to be labeled as angry or aggressive, which hinders their success (Correll, 2017). Ironically, research shows that employers that have higher tendencies toward a masculinity culture can have negative consequences for employees across the board, not just for female employees.

A high-masculinity culture is related to the presence of abusive leaders, low levels of psychological safety that prevent employees from expressing their ideas, low levels of work-life support, sexism, low levels of employees' physical and mental well-being, and higher turnover rates and burnout (Glick, Berdahl, & Alonso, 2018). It can also be related to gender harassment involving a hostile environment that is abusive and does not value women, as well as other forms of sexual harassment. Half of women faculty in STEM report that they have experienced gender harassment (Novotney,

2019). Organizations in STEM especially need to pay attention to the level of masculinity culture in their organizations and address these issues in order to retain and advance women.

- **Implement change strategies such as (1) encouraging members to adopt collective goals that support communal values and (2) establishing women's support networks and leadership forums.**

To combat a high-masculinity culture, organizations can identify collective goals that advance the firm's mission (Berdahl et al., 2018) to help change the culture. For example, in a study of an oil company, researchers (Ely & Meyerson, 2010) reported how the company discouraged having a high-masculinity culture while trying to improve the safety of the oil rig workers. By tying safety to the company's mission, the organization created an environment where overly masculine dysfunctional behaviors were not compatible with behaviors that improve safety; workers had to express doubts, behaviors that are usually incompatible with strong masculinity cultures. Employees were encouraged to "watch out for each other" instead of competing, "put several heads together" to solve problems instead of proving who is the winner, "admit mistakes" to prevent future mistakes, and "open up" to share personal problems that might interfere with their work. The company not only succeeded in improving worker safety but also in turning an extreme masculinity culture into one that values collective goals (Ely & Meyerson, 2010).

Creating an effective women's network to foster inclusion and culture change is another way to improve the retention of women in STEM. For example, Nokia (Di-Toro, 2018; Nokia.com, n.d.) has an award-winning, employee-driven women's network program called StrongHer to empower women and maximize women's contributions. StrongHer has been established in more than sixty countries with more than 2,000 members, including male employees (23 percent). StrongHer has four main programs. StrongHer awards is a recognition program highlighting women leaders' accomplishments. KIW-e* (Knowledge, Information and Wisdom for employees) encourages innovation through mentoring. KIW-e* webcasts widely communicate the knowledge and experience of leaders across the company. Charters for Managers foster managers' commitment to gender inclusion and championship by having them sign on to principles.

3M has also been a leader in women's leadership development, support networks, and workplace flexibility by establishing the "I'm In: Accelerating Women's Leadership" initiative and the Women's Leadership Forum in 2012 (HumanResources, 2017). This initiative helped 3M increase women's leadership roles at the director level from 18.2 percent to 23 percent and at the vice-president and above level from 16.7 percent to 24.2 percent in five years. The Women's Leadership Forum has now expanded to more than seventy-nine chapters around the world. Each chapter develops customized plans that fit the needs of their context.

In summary, a common aspect of Nokia's and 3M's efforts that have resulted in their success in creating a more supportive STEM organizational culture is that the organizations both share a strong commitment to enhancing gender inclusion. Both companies have set firm and measurable goals to achieve gender inclusion and have implemented strategic programs that send a strong message to employees that gender inclusion is closely tied to their core mission and that they are committed to achieving gender inclusion.

• **Address the gender pay gap that exists in STEM occupations.**
Another way to retain female employees in the STEM fields is to measure gender equality in the organization in terms of the gender pay gap and take action to remedy inequities. Women make 49 cents (Rose & Hartmann, 2018) to 80 cents for every dollar men make (Vagins, n.d.); and the gender pay gaps are often very large in STEM fields. Intel's actions provide an example of steps that can be taken to address the gender pay gap. Intel closed the gender and racial pay gap for employees in the United States in 2017 and

globally in early 2019 (Hinchliffe, 2019). Intel achieved this objective by tracking pay and promotion gaps by gender and race, as well as the retention rate of underrepresented minorities (Brown, 2017). Organizations can also focus their efforts to address the gender pay gap by identifying where the gender pay gap is most evident and then give raises to the identified employees, rather than across-the-board raises (Anderson et al., 2019).

An innovative strategy to achieve gender pay equality is to stop using prior salary history to set the current pay of new employees when they are hired (Vagins, n.d.). Because women are being paid less, using the previous salary at another firm as a starting point perpetuates the problem of institutionalized pay inequity. Moreover, studies show that women who fail to disclose salary history in pay negotiations for a new job are likely to receive offers that are 1.8 percent lower than women who did disclose past salary. Failure to disclose previous salary did not harm men's pay (Frank, 2017). Consequently, many states in the United States (as of March 2019 in California, Connecticut, Delaware, Hawaii, Illinois, Massachusetts, Michigan, New Jersey, New York, Oregon, Pennsylvania, Vermont, and Wisconsin) have passed legislation banning organizations from asking for the salary history of potential employees (Vagins, n.d.). Regardless of local legislation, organizations can help close the pay gap, which is particularly an issue in the STEM fields, by making offers based on current compensation salary surveys regardless of gender.

REFERENCES

Anderson, D., Bjarnadóttir, M.V., Dezso, C., & Ross, D.G. (2019, 21 January). Why companies' attempts to close the gender pay gap often fail. *Harvard Business Review*. Retrieved from https://hbr.org/2019/01/why-companies-attempts-to-close-the-gender-pay-gap-often-fail.

Archie, T., Kogan, M., & Laursen, S. (n.d.). Do labmates matter? The relative importance of workplace climate and work-life satisfaction in women scientists' job satisfaction. *International Journal of Gender Science and Technology*. Retrieved from http://genderandset.open.ac.uk.

Bailyn, L. (2003). Academic careers and gender equity: Lessons learned from MIT. *Gender, Work, and Organizations, 10*(2), 137–53. https://doi.org/10.1111/1468-0432.00008.

Benschop, Y., & Brouns, M. (2003). Crumbling ivory towers: Academic organizing and its gender effects. *Gender, Work and Organization, 10*(2), 194–212. https://doi.org/10.1111/1468-0432.t01-1-00011.

Berdahl, J.L., Glick, P., & Cooper, M. (2018, 2 November). How masculinity contests undermine organizations, and what to do about it. *Harvard Business Review*. Retrieved from https://hbr.org/2018/11/how-masculinity-contests-undermine-organizations-and-what-to-do-about-it.

Bersin, J. (2013, 16 August). Employee retention now a big issue: Why the tide has turned. Retrieved from https://www.linkedin.com/pulse/20130816200159-131079-employee-retention-now-a-big-issue-why-the-tide-has-turned/.

Bilimoria, D., & Liang, X. (2012). *Gender equity in science and engineering: Advancing change in higher education*. New York: Routledge.

Bray, J.W., Hinde, J.M., Kaiser, D.J., Mills, M.J., Karuntzos, G.T., Genadek, K.R., ... & Hurtado, D.A. (2018). Effects of a flexibility/support intervention on work performance: Evidence from the Work, Family, and Health Network. *American Journal of Health Promotion, 32*(4), 963–70. https://doi.org/10.1177/0890117117696244.

Brown, D. (2017, 28 February). Intel's 2016 annual report. Retrieved from https://blogs.intel.com/csr/2017/02/annual-report-2016/.

Burrelli, J. (2008). InfoBrief: Thirty-three years of women in S&E faculty positions. National Science Foundation InfoBrief (NSF 08-308). Arlington, VA. Retrieved from https://wayback.archive-it.org/5902/20160210152800/http://www.nsf.gov/statistics/infbrief/nsf08308/.

Caton, M.T. (2007). Common trends in U.S. women college president issues. *Forum on Public Policy, 2007*(3), 0–25.

Cantor, N., Mack, K., McDermott, P., & Taylor, O. (2014). If not now, when? The promise of STEM intersectionality in the twenty-first century. *Peer Review*, *16*(2), 29–30.

Cheryan, S., Ziegler, S.A., Montoya, A.K., & Jiang, L. (2017). Why are some STEM fields more gender balanced than others? *Psychological Bulletin*, *143*(1), 1–35. https://doi.org/10.1037/bul0000052.

Correll, S.J. (2017). SWS 2016 Feminist lecture: Reducing gender biases in modern workplaces: A small wins approach to organizational change. *Gender & Society*, *31*(6), 725–50. https://doi.org/10.1177/0891243217738518.

Crain, T.L., Hammer, L.B., Bodner, T., Kossek, E.E., Moen, P., Lilienthal, R., & Buxton, O.M. (2014). Work–family conflict, family-supportive supervisor behaviors (FSSB), and sleep outcomes. *Journal of Occupational Health Psychology*, *19*(2), 155–67. https://doi.org/10.1037/t23690-000.

Curie, M. (1923). *Pierre Curie with autobiographical notes by Marie Curie*. New York: Macmillan.

Dean, D.J., & Fleckenstein, A. (2007). Keys to success for women in science. In R.J. Burke & M.C. Mattis (Eds.), *Women and minorities in science, technology, engineering and mathematics*, 28–46. Cheltenham: Edward Elgar.

Di-Toro, M. (2018). Nokia's head of diversity: How we leveled the playing field for women in STEM. Retrieved from https://www.glassdoor.com/employers/blog/nokia/.

Durham, C.M. (2000). Gender and professional identity: Unexplored issues in judicial performance evaluation. *Judges' Journal*, *39*, 11–12.

Ely, R.J., & Kimmel, M. (2018). Thoughts on the workplace as a masculinity contest. *Journal of Social Issues*, *74*(3), 628–34. https://doi.org/10.1111/josi.12290.

Ely, R.J., & Meyerson, D.E. (2010). An organizational approach to undoing gender: The unlikely case of offshore oil platforms. *Research in Organizational Behavior*, *30*, 3–34. https://doi.org/10.1016/j.riob.2010.09.002.

Fox, M.F. (2010). Women and men faculty in academic science and engineering: Social-organizational indicators and implications. *American Behavioral Scientist, 53*(7), 997–1012. https://doi.org/10.1177/0002764209356234.

Frank, L. (2017, 5 September). Why banning questions about salary history may not improve pay equity. *Harvard Business Review*. Retrieved from https://hbr.org/2017/09/why-banning-questions-about-salary-history-may-not-improve-pay-equity.

Gallup. (2017). State of the American workplace. Gallup. Retrieved from https://www.gallup.com/workplace/238085/state-american-workplace-report-2017.aspx.

Glick, P., Berdahl, J.L., & Alonso, N.M. (2018). Development and validation of the masculinity contest culture scale. *Journal of Social Issues, 74*(3), 449–76. https://doi.org/10.1111/josi.12280.

Goulden, M., Frasch, K., & Mason, M. (2009). *Staying competitive: Patching America's leaky pipeline in the sciences*. Washington, DC: Center for American Progress.

Hammer, L.B., Kossek, E.E., Anger, W.K., Bodner, T., & Zimmerman, K.L. (2011). Clarifying work-family intervention processes: The roles of work-family conflict and family-supportive supervisor behaviors. *Journal of Applied Psychology, 96*(1), 134–50. https://doi.org/10.1037/a0020927.

Hammer, L.B., Truxillo, D.M., Bodner, T., Rineer, J., Pytlovany, A.C., & Richman, A. (2015). Effects of a workplace intervention targeting psychosocial risk factors on safety and health outcomes. *Biomed Research International, 2015*, 1–12. https://doi.org/10.1155/2015/836967.

Heilman, M.E., Wallen, A.S., Fuchs, D., & Tamkins, M.M. (2004). Penalties for success: Reactions to women who succeed at male gender-typed tasks. *Journal of Applied Psychology, 89*(3), 416–27. https://doi.org/10.1037/0021-9010.89.3.416.

Hinchliffe, E. (2019, 22 January). Intel just closed its pay gap again – this time taking stock into account. Retrieved from http://fortune.com/2019/01/22/intel-gender-pay-gap-stock/.

Hollenshead, C. (2007). Women in the academy: Confronting barriers to equality. In L.S. Hornig (Ed.), *Equal rites, unequal outcomes: Women in American research universities,* 211–26. New York: Kluwer Academic /Plenum Publishers.

HumanResources. (2017, 18 September). Case study: How 3M is accelerating women in leadership. Retrieved from https://www .humanresourcesonline.net/case-study-how-3m-is-accelerating-women -in-leadership/.

Kelly, E.L., Moen, P., Oakes, J.M., Fan, W., Okechukwu, C., Davis, K.D., ... & Casper, L.M. (2014). Changing work and work-family conflict: Evidence from the Work, Family, and Health Network. *American Sociological Review, 79*(3), 485–516. http://doi.org/10.1177 /0003122414531435.

Kossek, E.E., & Hammer, L. (2008). Work/life training for supervisors gets big results. *Harvard Business Review, 36.* Retrieved from https://hbr. org/2008/11/supervisor-worklife-training-gets-results.

Kossek, E.E., Hammer, L.B., Kelly, E.L., & Moen, P. (2014). Designing work, family & health organizational change initiatives. *Organizational Dynamics, 43*(1), 53–63. http://doi.org/10.1016/j.orgdyn.2013.10.007.

Kossek, E.E., Petty, R.J., Bodner, T.E., Perrigino, M.B., Hammer, L.B., Yragui, N.L., & Michel, J.S. (2018). Lasting impression: Transformational leadership and family supportive supervision as resources for well-being and performance. *Occupational Health Science, 2*(1), 1–24. https:// doi.org/10.1007/s41542-018-0012-x.

Kossek, E.E., Pichler, S., Bodner, T., & Hammer, L.B. (2011). Workplace social support and work-family conflict: A meta-analysis clarifying the influence of general and work-family-specific supervisor and organizational support. *Personnel Psychology, 64*(2), 289–313. https:// doi.org/10.1111/j.1744-6570.2011.01211.x.

Laurent-Ottomane, C. (2012). Gender diversity on corporate boards: The thirty percent coalition and the critical mass effect. Sustainable Brands. Retrieved from http://www.sustainablebrands.com/news_and_views /new-metrics/corporate-boards-more-women-enhance-governance.

Mack, K., Rankins, C., & Winston, C. (2011). Black women faculty at historically Black colleges and universities: Perspectives for a national imperative. In H. Frierson & W. Tate (Eds.), *Beyond stock stories and folktales: African Americans' paths to STEM fields (Diversity in Higher Education, Volume 11)*, 149–64. London: Emerald Group Publishing Limited.

Mack, K., Rankins, C., & Woodson, K. (2013). From graduate school to the STEM workforce: An entropic approach to career identity development for STEM women of color. *New Directions for Higher Education, 2013*(163), 23–34. https://doi.org/10.1002/he.20062.

Mack, K., Taylor, O., Cantor, N., & McDermott, P. (2014). If not now, when? The promise of STEM intersectionality in the twenty-first century. *Peer Review, 16*, 29–31. Retrieved from https://www.aacu.org/publications-research/periodicals/if-not-now-when-promise-stem-intersectionality-twenty-first.

Mackenzie, L., Wehner, J., & Correll, S. (2019, 11 January). Why most performance evaluations are biased, and how to fix them. *Harvard Business Review*. Retrieved from https://hbr.org/2019/01/why-most-performance-evaluations-are-biased-and-how-to-fix-them.

MacNell, L., Driscoll, A., & Hunt, A.N. (2015). What's in a name: Exposing gender bias in student ratings of teaching. *Innovative Higher Education, 40*(4), 291–303. https://doi.org/10.1007/s10755-014-9313-4.

Malcom, L., & Malcom, M. (2011). The double bind: The next generation. *Harvard Educational Review, 81* (2), 162–72. https://doi.org/10.17763/haer.81.2.a84201x508406327.

Malcom, S.M., Hall, P.Q., & Brown, J.W. (1976). *The double bind: The price of being a minority woman in science*. Washington, DC: American Association for the Advancement of Science.

Massachusetts Institute of Technology. (1999). A study on the status of women faculty in science at MIT. Massachusetts, MA: MIT. Retrieved from http://web.mit.edu/fnl/women/women.pdf.

Mendoza, E., & Johnson, K. (2000). *Land of plenty: Diversity of America's competitive edge in science, engineering and technology*. Report of the

Congressional Commission on the Advancement of Women and Minorities in Science, Engineering and Technology Development, National Science Foundation.

National Academies. (2007a). *Beyond bias and barriers: Fulfilling the potential of women in academic science and engineering.* Washington, DC: National Academies Press.

National Academies. (2007b). *Rising above the gathering storm: Energizing and employing America for a brighter economic future.* Washington, DC: National Academies Press.

National Science Foundation, Division of Science Resources Statistics. (2015). *Women, minorities, and persons with disabilities in science and engineering: 2015.* NSF 15-311. Arlington, VA. Retrieved from https://www.nsf.gov/publications/pub_summ.jsp?ods_key=nsf15311.

Nokia.com. (n.d.). StrongHer. Retrieved from https://www.nokia.com/about-us/sustainability/strongher/.

Novotney, A. (2019). Renewing the push for equality. *Monitor on Psychology, 50,* 36–44.

Ong, M., Wright, C., Espinosa, L., & Orfield, G. (2010). Inside the double bind: A synthesis of empirical research on women of color in science, technology, engineering, and mathematics. National Science Foundation (NSF-DRL #0635577).

Page, S.E. (2007). Making the difference: Applying a logic of diversity. *The Academy of Management Perspectives, 21*(4), 6–20. https://doi.org/10.5465/amp.2007.27895335.

Rankins, C., Rankins, F., & Inniss, T. (2014). Who is minding the gap? *Peer Review, 16,* 2. Retrieved from https://www.aacu.org/peerreview/2014/spring/rankins.

Rose, S.J., & Hartman, H.I. (2018). Still a man's labor market: The slowly narrowing gender wage gap. Institute for Women's Policy Research. Retrieved from https://iwpr.org/publications/still-mans-labor-market/.

Rosser, S. (2004). *The science glass ceiling: Academic women scientists and the struggle to succeed.* New York: Routledge.

Rudman, L.A., Moss-Racusin, C.A., Phelan, J.E., & Nauts, S. (2012). Status incongruity and backlash effects: Defending the gender hierarchy motivates prejudice against female leaders. *Journal of Experimental Social Psychology, 48*(1), 165–79. https://doi.org/10.1016/j.jesp.2011.10.008.

Sanchez-Hucles, J., & Davis, D. (2010). Women and women of color in leadership: Complexity, identity, and intersectionality. *American Psychologist, 65*(3), 171–81. https://doi.org/10.1037/a0017459.

Silbey, S.S. (2016, 23 August). Why do so many women who study engineering leave the field? *Harvard Business Review*. Retrieved from https://hbr.org/2016/08/why-do-so-many-women-who-study -engineering-leave-the-field.

Silver, B., Boudreaux-Bartels, G., Mederer, H., Pasquerella, L.C., Peckham, J., River-Hudec, M., & Wishner, K. (2006). A warmer climate for women in engineering at the University of Rhode Island. 2006 Annual Conference Proceedings Paper, American Society for Engineering Education. Retrieved from https://peer.asee.org/a-warmer-climate -for-women-in-engineering.

Snipes, R.L., Thomson, N.F., & Oswald, S.L. (2006). Gender bias in customer evaluations of service quality: An empirical investigation. *Journal of Services Marketing, 20*(4), 274–84. https://doi.org/10.1108 /08876040610674616.

Steinpreis, R.E., Anders, K.A., & Ritzke, D. (1999). The impact of gender on the review of the curricula vitae of job applicants and tenure candidates: A national empirical study. *Sex Roles, 41*(7–8), 509–28. https://doi.org/10.1023/A:1018839203698.

Taylor, O., & Mack, K. (2015, April). Academic leadership and the enhancement of access and equity in STEM. Presentation at Gender Summit 5, Cape Town, South Africa.

Transforming Women's Leadership. (2016, 21 July). Deloitte's predictability and flexibility initiative pays dividends in work/life balance. Thomson Reuters. Retrieved from http://www.legalexecutiveinstitute.com /deloittes-flexibility-initiative/.

Truth, S. (1851, December). Ain't I a Women? A speech at Women's
Convention, Akron, Ohio.

Uhlmann, E., & Cohen, G.L. (2005). Constructed criteria: Redefining merit
to justify discrimination. *Psychological Science, 16*(6), 474–80. https://
doi.org/10.1111/j.0956-7976.2005.01559.x.

U.S. Department of Labor. (2007). *The STEM workforce challenge: The role
of the public workforce system in a national solution for a competitive science,
technology, engineering, and mathematics (STEM) workforce.* Washington,
DC: Department of Labor. Retrieved from https://digitalcommons.ilr
.cornell.edu/key_workplace/637/.

Vagins, D.J. (n.d.). The simple truth about the gender pay gap. Retrieved
from https://www.aauw.org/research/the-simple-truth-about-the
-gender-pay-gap/.

Valian, V. (2004). Beyond gender schemas: Improving the advancement
of women in academia. *National Women's Studies Association Journal, 16,*
207–20. https://doi.org/10.1111/j.1527-2001.2005.tb00495.x.

Zukin, C., & Szeltner, M. (2012). Talent report: What workers want in 2012.
Net Impact. Retrieved from www.netimpact.org/whatworkerswant.

6

LEARNING FROM ENTREPRENEURIAL SETTINGS

Life-fulfilling work is never about the money – when you feel true passion for something you instinctively find ways to nurture it.

– Eileen Fisher, fashion designer/retailer and founder of Eileen Fisher, Inc.

What the Research Tells Us: The Glass Ceiling of Entrepreneurship and How Some Women Are Breaking Free

KIMBERLY EDDLESTON

Around the globe, more and more women are taking their careers in their own hands by launching a business. Women represent one of the fastest-growing segments of the entrepreneurship population worldwide (GEM, 2013; Jennings & Brush, 2013; Zarya, 2015). For example, in the United States, the number of women-owned businesses grew by 59 percent between 1997 and 2013, which is about one-and-a-half times the national average (American Express, 2013). An article in *Fortune* points out that across all ethnicities, the number of women-owned businesses is increasing faster than that of men-owned businesses. Since 2007 the number of businesses owned by White women has increased by 10.1 percent, those by Asian women by 44.3 percent, those by Black women by 667.5 percent, and those by Hispanic women by 87.5 percent (Zarya, 2015). Further, world-wide, women own approximately 25 to 33 percent of all private businesses, according to the World Bank. In sub-Saharan Africa, Latin America, and developing Asian countries, women's rate of entrepreneurship is almost on a par with that of men (GEM, 2013). Additionally, women are making great strides in their develop-ment of innovative products and services, with women outpacing men in the United States and parts of Asia (GEM, 2013). Since the recent recession, women have also been shown to have increased their net employment, while male entrepreneurs tended to cut jobs (American Express, 2013). This surge in women's entrepreneurship led the *Economist* to exclaim, "Forget China, India and the internet: economic growth is driven by women" (*Economist*, 2006).

Despite these gains, however, on average women are still less likely to engage in entrepreneurship than men (Jennings & Brush, 2013; Kelley, Brush, Greene, & Litovsky, 2011), and their businesses' average revenues, profitability, and assets are lower than those of male entrepreneurs (Davis & Shaver, 2012; Gupta, Turban, & Pareek, 2013; Hughes, Jennings, Brush, Carter, & Welter, 2012; Jennings & Brush, 2013). Fewer than 20 percent of U.S. women-owned busi-nesses' revenues exceeded $100,000 annually, in comparison to 32 percent of businesses owned by men. Although women own approximately 30 percent of America's privately held firms, they employ just 14 percent of the nation's private-sector workforce and receive only 11 percent of private-sector revenues (American Express, 2013). It appears that women tend to start their businesses with fewer capital resources than men and that differences in capi-talization persist over the life of the business (Carter, Brush, Greene, Gatewood, & Hart, 2003; Jennings & Brush, 2013). As a result, the businesses owned by women are smaller, less profitable, and slower growing than those owned by men (Cliff, 1998; Jennings & Brush, 2013). This has led some to question if entrepreneurship is yet an-other career path with a glass ceiling for women and if the glass ceiling is created by discriminatory practices or self-imposed limits to success.

In this essay, I will review some of the latest research on women entrepreneurs, focusing first on barriers that appear to limit their success, and second on ways that women entrepreneurs have shattered the glass ceiling, or in some instances, redefined entrepreneurship, thus making the proverbial glass ceiling obsolete. Finally, given the increasing number of women leading family businesses and being considered as successors (EY Report, 2015), I will also discuss the unique barriers and opportunities that exist for women working in their family's business. The essay concludes with implications for future research and practice.

The Gendered Lens of Entrepreneurship

Entrepreneurship has traditionally been depicted as a male preserve, with the entrepreneur being described as a "captain of industry" (Schumpeter, 1934), "heroic self-made man" (Ahl, 2006), and "conqueror of unexplored territories" (Bruni, Gherardi, & Poggio, 2004). Entrepreneurs are commonly described as aggressive, ambitious risk-takers, trailblazers, and patriarchs, an image that has led to a masculine view of entrepreneurship (Ahl, 2002; Bruni et al., 2004). As such, in discussions of successful entrepreneurs, a male stereotype persists (Eddleston, Ladge, Mitteness, & Balachandra, 2016). This stereotype is further fostered by the greater prevalence of men than of women in positions of power and authority (Powell, 2011) and the fact that most entrepreneurial role models are men (BarNir, Watson, & Hutchins, 2011; Gupta, Turban, Wasti, & Sikdar, 2009). Because of the masculine lens of entrepreneurship, when women choose to become entrepreneurs, they are perceived as less legitimate, less serious, and less committed business owners (Eddleston et al., 2016). For example, capital providers tend to view women's businesses as hobbies, part-time work, or an extension of their homemaker's role, a view that leads them to be perceived as poor investments (Arenius & Autio, 2006; Loscocco & Smith-Hunter, 2004). This masculine view of entrepreneurship, by both men and women (Gupta et al., 2009), is likely why many women believe that they lack the skills and capacity to succeed as entrepreneurs (Wilson, Kickul, & Marlino, 2007). It has also hurt their ability to access resources that are essential to entrepreneurial success (Eddleston et al., 2016; Jennings & Brush, 2013).

Businesses owned by women are persistently smaller, slower growing, and less profitable than those owned by men (Jennings & Brush, 2013; Loscocco & Bird, 2012; Powell & Eddleston, 2013). Common reasons given for this disparity are the lower levels of job inputs and resources that women versus men contribute to their businesses, such as education, work experience, and financial and social capital (Carter & Williams, 2003; Menzies, Diochon, & Gasse, 2004; Powell & Eddleston, 2008). For instance, women tend to launch their businesses with less financing than men (Carter et al., 2003; Fairlie & Robb, 2009), and significantly fewer women seek angel investment than men (Becker-Blease & Sohl, 2007). Another reason for the gender disparity in entrepreneurial success is that businesses tend to be gendered in nature, in that women often own businesses in consumer-oriented retail and personal service industries that have limited growth, as opposed to industries associated with manufacturing and technology (Fairlie & Robb, 2009; Gupta et al., 2009; Kelley et al., 2011; Morris, Miyasaki, Watters, & Coombes, 2006). Finally, women-owned businesses may be smaller, slower-growing, and less profitable because of discriminatory practices and covert biases that create barriers for them (Eddleston et al., 2016). Indeed, recent research shows that banks hold women entrepreneurs to a different standard than their male counterparts when awarding loans (Eddleston et al., 2016). Banks have also been found to charge female entrepreneurs higher interest rates than they charge male entrepreneurs, providing evidence of a more subtle and "second-order" form of gender discrimination (Wu & Chua, 2012). Interestingly, however, some evidence suggests that the disparities in business performance are reduced when specific control variables are considered, such as industry, business age, and business size (Robb & Watson, 2012; Watson & Robinson, 2003). Thus, it appears that women entrepreneurs may have started to narrow the business performance gap (Davis & Shaver, 2012; Jennings & Brush, 2013; Powell & Eddleston, 2013).

Women Entrepreneurs: Creating Their Own Definition of Success

While there is much research that compares the business success of male and female entrepreneurs, scholars have criticized this work for its dependence on a male definition of success that emphasizes status and financial achievements. These scholars have called for a new, feminine lens of entrepreneurship that considers women's goals and preferences as well as the outcomes they seek from entrepreneurship (Bruni et al., 2004; Brush, 1992; Eddleston & Powell, 2008). They also call for research to explore how "doing" entrepreneurship is gendered; that is, how men and women may lead and manage their businesses in different ways. For example, male entrepreneurs tend to highly value financial rewards, status, and "getting ahead," and female entrepreneurs tend to place greater value on building relationships with employees and customers and on balancing work and family (Brush, 1992; DeMartino & Barbato, 2003; Eddleston & Powell, 2008). Further, although research shows that men place greater emphasis on status and women place greater emphasis on socio-emotional sources of career satisfaction, such as relationships with employees and contributing to society, it also shows that gender identity – that is, the degree to which an entrepreneur possesses masculine and feminine traits – has a stronger influence on their sources of satisfaction than does biological sex (Eddleston & Powell, 2008). Such findings not only demonstrate how entrepreneurship is a gendered process but also highlight the variance in entrepreneurial goals and values among men and women.

Research exploring the different values and goals of male and female entrepreneurs (i.e., DeMartino & Barbato, 2003; Eddleston & Powell, 2008; Morris et al., 2006) led Powell and Eddleston (2008) to propose and test the existence of a "paradox of the contented female business owner." This paradox captures the fact that women entrepreneurs apparently experience career satisfaction despite having lower sales, slower growth, and lower profits than their male counterparts. Evidence for the paradox of the contented female business owner was strongly provided, and the study revealed that the paradox was best explained by gender differences in what men and women value from entrepreneurship versus differential job inputs. Further, the study showed that women business owners' career satisfaction was less sensitive to fluctuations in business performance and sales in comparison to that of men. This finding may help explain why male entrepreneurs are much more interested in growing their businesses than are women. Studies repeatedly show that women are less interested in business expansion and growth than their male counterparts (Carter et al., 2003; Cliff, 1998; Davis & Shaver, 2012; Kelley et al., 2011). In particular, Cliff's (1998) study revealed that women are more likely than men to set a maximum business-size threshold for their firms that they will not surpass. For women, therefore, business growth is a deliberate choice.

In considering why women are more likely to limit the size and growth of their business, researchers tend to highlight differences in the work-family interface for men and women (i.e., Davis & Shaver, 2012; Goffee & Scase, 1985; Jennings & McDougald, 2007). Brush's (1992) seminal article highlights the "integrated perspective" of women entrepreneurs, whereby they tend to view their businesses as integrated with other aspects of their lives, particularly their family. Studies in this vein show that women often start their own businesses in the hope of better balancing their work and family lives (Chaganti,

1986; Collins-Dodd, Gordon, & Smart, 2004; DeMartino & Barbato, 2003), although, in reality, women entrepreneurs struggle to achieve such balance (Loscocco, Robinson, Hall, & Allen, 1991; Shelton, 2006). In applying a gendered perspective to the work-family balance of entrepreneurs, Eddleston and Powell (2012) found that satisfaction with work-family balance is nurtured in different ways by men and women. Women expressed greater satisfaction with work-family balance when they created synergies between the two domains through instrumental family-to-business enrichment, and men expressed greater satisfaction with work-family balance when they received higher levels of family support at home. This study, therefore, suggests that the family nurtures entrepreneurship in gendered ways.

In further exploring how the family can enrich entrepreneurship, Powell and Eddleston (2013) extended theory on family enrichment and support to investigate gender differences in how one's family can contribute to entrepreneurial success. Their study revealed that female entrepreneurs benefit from family-to-business enrichment and support more than men do, suggesting that women are best able to capitalize on family-based resources. Although the positive link between family enrichment and support and entrepreneurial success for women could be partially due to their lack of access to other resources, such as human, social, and financial capital, this study uncovered a unique resource that women appear best able to apply to their businesses. Similarly, a study by Cruz and colleagues (2012) showed that women entrepreneurs are better able to leverage the benefits of kinship ties than are their male counterparts; that is, the employment of family members leads to a greater increase in sales for female business owners in comparison to male business owners. Studies like this highlight how the family is integral to women's entrepreneurial success and may be key to shattering remnants of the glass ceiling that persists. Accordingly, we now turn to discuss women in family businesses and the role of gender in family business leadership.

Women in Family Business: Another Glass Ceiling to Shatter?

As women are increasingly taking part in the business world and launching their own businesses, they are also becoming more active and visible in family businesses (Dugan, Krone, LeCouvie, Pendergast, Kenyon-Rouvinez, & Schuman, 2011). A recent EY Report on the world's largest family businesses found that 41 percent of the firms surveyed recognized female family members' increasing interest in joining their family business. They also found that 70 percent of the firms were considering a woman for their next CEO and 55 percent had at least one woman on their board. Further, 24 percent of family firms are led by a female CEO or president, and almost 60 percent have women in top management positions (Mass Mutual, 2007). In comparison, only 2.5 percent of non-family firms in the *Fortune* 1000 are led by a woman. Nelton (1998) forecasts that by 2023, one-third of America's family businesses will be run by a woman if family business leadership trends match those of entrepreneurship in the United States. If family businesses embrace women's leadership, they may be paramount in shattering the glass ceiling, since the vast majority of firms around the globe are family businesses, and approximately 35 percent of *Fortune* 500 companies are under family control.

Unfortunately, however, women in family businesses are often subject to the same biases and gender-based discrimination as women in business. For example, a 2015 study of German family businesses showed that males are still preferred over females for CEO succession and that females require much greater human capital than their male counterparts to be chosen as a successor (Ahrens, Landmann, & Woywode, 2015). Often a woman is chosen as a CEO successor only when no son exists to lead the family business. In the United Kingdom and France, approximately two-thirds of family businesses choose their next CEO by primogeniture (Bloom & Van Reenen, 2007). Therefore, although some believe that women have more career options and leadership opportunities in family businesses than in non-family businesses (Cole, 1997; Salganicoff, 1990), for the CEO position, it appears that family businesses still prefer a male family heir (Ahrens et al., 2015).

Besides the CEO-level glass ceiling, family businesses also appear to discriminate against women in some of their employment practices. For example, Rowe & Hong (2000) found that many women working in their family's business did not receive salaries, or they were paid significantly less than men. Family businesses appear to take advantage of female family members as a result of gender norms in the family that emphasize women's roles as supporters and nurturers (Freudenberger, Freedheim, & Kurtz, 1989). However, family business scholars have acknowledged how women's support for their family's business is often instrumental in the business's survival and success, particularly during the early years of the business and times of growth (Danes, Haberman, & McTavish, 2005; Jimenez, 2009). Furthermore, as women's roles continue to evolve, more and more are achieving leadership positions in their family businesses (Dugan et al., 2011). In turn, those family businesses that welcome and appreciate women's involvement appear to garner the most success, as suggested in the EY Report. Therefore, while family businesses appear to have a unique glass ceiling that inhibits the appreciation and advancement of women because of traditional gender role norms that traverse from the family to the business domain, there are signs that progress is being made.

Conclusion and Future Directions

Entrepreneurship offers women the unique opportunity to define their own career path and success. As a career, entrepreneurship offers a degree of autonomy, self-fulfillment, and independence that few other careers can provide. Women entrepreneurs are able to create businesses that uniquely meet their needs and allow them to pursue personally defined goals and strategies (Bird & Brush, 2002). Family businesses are also starting to acknowledge women's contributions to their success, with an increasing number of family businesses around the globe promoting women into top management positions (EY Report, 2015). Further, research recognizes the growing number of family firms that are started and led by women (Mass Mutual, 2007). Such advances have led to the declaration that "entrepreneurship is the new women's movement" (MacNeil, 2012).

Around the world, the role of women entrepreneurs in growing their country's economy and job creation is being recognized. Efforts to promote women's entrepreneurship, like the 10,000 Women Initiative, have successfully demonstrated how training and education contribute to women entrepreneurs' success, especially in emerging markets. The 10,000 Women Initiative is a program developed by Goldman Sachs to help underserved women entrepreneurs globally through business education, mentoring, and access to capital. To date, they have helped more than 10,000 women entrepreneurs in fifty-six countries. Yet, while progress is being made, there are still countries where women are not allowed to launch a business unless they receive permission from the male head of their family (Sullivan & Meek, 2012). To fully dismantle the glass ceiling on women's entrepreneurship, it is thus necessary to make progress in promoting women's equality throughout the world. Once entrepreneurship as a career path is a possibility for all women, each can then decide how to manage and lead her business so that it best contributes to her individually prescribed definition of success.

Moving forward, researchers need to acknowledge the diversity among female entrepreneurs and not subject them to male definitions of success. Additionally, as acceptance of the feminine model of entrepreneurship continues to grow, men should be encouraged to consider embracing feminine definitions of success and styles of management. A greater appreciation for women's innate strengths and leadership-style tendencies will also likely contribute to greater gender equality in family businesses. My hope is that this essay will encourage further research on the promise of women's entrepreneurship around the globe and inspire women entrepreneurs to continue to chip away at the glass ceiling so that they can eventually "send the elevator back down" to the next generation of women leaders.

View from Practice: Emerging Organizational Culture and Inclusion

NINA SWANSON

I work in a company where innovation is our life. The company is about twenty years old, and in that time we have grown from a firm of 2 people to 17,000 people globally. The company was acquired in 2002 by a bigger firm. It was a mutually beneficial relationship for both companies. The company grew substantially through the bigger firm and its customers. Now we are going through a fairly radical transformation as a company. Because of divergent strategies, and where we were going as companies, a decision was made that the two companies will separate. Because of this change, we are in a unique position as a company. It gives us a chance to redefine our path forward as a company. It is incredibly important for employees to continue to look at who we are and where we are trying to go.

There are many improvements related to diversity at the company. First, we have seen a significant increase in the number of women in leadership roles. It amazes me to know that by starting to say that we need to get better at something, we actually can get better at it. By talking about it, we also started doing things differently. We strive for parity in the gender composition of our company – that is 50/50. Still, we have parts of our business that are not yet 50/50. Global operations tend to be fairly female, and we have a pretty good parity there. Traditionally female occupations such as legal HR have good parity. Even on the marketing side of our business, we might have become a little bit closer. But we have got to get better.

There are several things we have implemented to help women in our company. We have expanded our maternity benefits for men and women. We are making policy changes that are not just for women but that benefit both men and women. What we have seen so far is that men realize that it is very helpful to them. I have not anticipated it, but the responses from the men, regardless of generation, are very encouraging. Additionally, we started a program to help women who have been out of the field for a while, mainly because of child-bearing. We started it in India, and we are bringing it to the United States. In India, most women tend to stay at home after having a baby. With our six-week product cycle, if you leave for any length of time, you can lose your edge on just the software engineering side. We give them eighteen weeks of an on-boarding experience to get them up to speed on where they left and where we are now, so that they can jump right in and start doing the work again.

We also have a global program to get female students to be involved in coding. For us, it is a pipeline activity to close the gender gaps in technology education. We want to get girls to get excited about computer science. We are also partnering with a renowned research center to understand unconscious bias in performance reviews. We have improved our approach to college recruiting and increasing our college hires. It is, without a doubt, a significant help for both genders as well as for broader diversity dimensions to have robust college recruiting. We want to create an exciting place that people want to come to work in.

However, there are challenges. The company is a financial technology company, which is different from a payment center. It means that we are bringing technology into a platform that is much broader than just payments such as credit and remittances. The company will continue to grow, not only by what we provide to our customers but by the acquisitions. As we were separating from the bigger firm, we were also acquiring three large companies at the same time. These acquisitions mean that we suddenly have three different cultures and expectations. We have different ways of working that are going to constantly be coming into our business, and we are struggling with many questions. How much is too much culture? How much will drive away people who join a start-up? People from a small start-up company we acquired consider us a big bad brother. This is new for us. We always thought of ourselves as an innovative start-up. It seems that we are not an innovative start-up anymore.

Moreover, the pace of our company is fast. Our website is a completely new site every six weeks, involving thousands of engineering hours. Thus, the pace at which we must innovate is measured in what we do not in eighteen months but in about thirty days. The pace also then translates to our employee experience. Our jobs are fluid. We have new jobs every sixty to ninety days. We currently have almost 100 vice-presidents, and only two of them have the same job they had a year ago. The rest of them have all got new responsibilities. In an environment where people are constantly changing positions, how do we give people a sense of career progression? How do we give them a sense of career development? Defining career is very different in this environment, and it is a big challenge.

In a tech company, what you get rewarded for is based on what you develop versus how you do it. We need to build relationships and a much stronger bench of people leaders; this is especially important for all employees but especially for women. We have not focused on people leaders yet. We have focused on whether you get cool buttons on the site. We get excited when you make a mobile app look awesome. We do not get excited when you read that somebody grows into another role. We are figuring out ways to create dual paths where we can get some really great people leaders and, at the same time, reward them for their technical capability. We focus a lot on our customers, and rightly so. However, we are also constantly looking at ways of creating an employee experience that is as profound and robust as the customer experience we strive for.

How do we create those robust experiences from the employees' perspective? Based on these improvements and challenges, we believe this is our time to define our culture in a way that engages the hearts and minds of all of our employees and to begin building a sense of who we are. If employees believe in the passion and mission about who we are, they will have a place to be successful. We are planning to spend a lot of time in the next year looking at our mission and our values and our culture. We asked our employees what was the experience that our employees want, and they came up with four great ideas. First, they want to have feedback about how they are doing periodically to know that they are on the right path. Employees can feel lost amid the fast pace and shifting projects and priorities, and feedback can help them feel anchored. Second, they want to have growth for themselves and growth for their team. It is not about the money or the title. They want to work on something that makes them better at what they do or helps them grow their skill set. Third, they want to be cared for. They want to know that somebody is interested in who they are as a person, where they want to go, and how they want to get there. Many leaders are really struggling with this because having those real conversations about what is important to somebody can be tricky and uncomfortable. Lastly, employees want to have trust. Trust is incredibly important in an environment where there is a lot of chaos.

Through a three-day workshop, employees came up with four anchors of who we are as a culture: collaboration, inclusion, wellness, and innovation. Employees brainstormed on where we have been, where we are going, what we like, and what we do not like. For now, this is a starting point. First is collaboration. We are an internet company. We do not have offices. Moreover, we also have many people like myself who work at home. Collaboration happens through video conferencing. We spend a lot of time in that space and are doing more of that across our business. Second is inclusion. As I mentioned previously, we try to create an inclusive place fostering diversity of thought. The third is wellness. We talk about work-life balance, and how we define work-life balance is very personal. Some people look at my schedule and say they do not understand how I keep up the pace I do. However, I feel just fine with my schedule. I have control of my schedule and my day. I work at home. I can go do my workout during the day when I do not need to be in my house. Two nights a week, I have to be on the phone until midnight because I need to connect with people in Singapore. However, I do not have to check in till late in the morning on those days. Thus, I feel I have a lot more flexibility. We are acknowledging that there are different ways that people are going to come to work. Fourth is innovation. We are talking a lot about innovation in terms of putting yourself in other people's shoes, which I call empathetic innovation. It is being crystal clear that the innovation you are proposing does not just come from within you but is also grounded in how you know others are experiencing it. Once again, while these concepts are critical to all workers, some of these themes – such as control over hours and flexibility – are especially critical for gender inclusion.

We do not have a clear answer as to where we will go with these concepts yet because they were developed very recently. We are just starting this work. Collaboration across functions has been huge throughout the process so far. What we are learning is that we will not be able to deliver for our customers if we do not work collaboratively across our functions and within our functions. We have built rewards around silos across which we function as every organization has. We are breaking down those silos and trying to see how that works for us as a company. We have a lot of work to do. However, it is an exciting time to be involved in doing it. Not many companies get to redefine themselves at this point in our career or at this point in our life. But we do, so it's great.

Integrating Research and Practice: Entrepreneurial Settings

NATHALIE DUVAL-COUETIL

Around the world, investments are being made in a wide range of initiatives designed to foster entrepreneurship and technological innovation in order to drive job creation and economic growth. Businesses with fewer than fifty employees account for 95 percent of all U.S. companies, ventures under five years old account for nearly all net job creation, and younger firms contribute to the vibrancy of the economy by injecting innovation and competition into existing markets. According to the Kauffman Foundation, a challenge for the U.S. economy is that the rate of new business start-ups has slowed significantly since its peak a decade ago, and for the first time business closures are now outpacing start-ups since researchers first started collecting data in the 1970s (Harrison, 2015; Kauffman Foundation, 2015). Among solutions that have been put forth to spur innovation and entrepreneurship is to be more inclusive of women in the development of human capital able to participate in entrepreneurship, and in technical fields, more generally (Mitchell, 2011).

It is clear that traditional models of work and career are changing rapidly. Organizations and communities are increasingly reliant on entrepreneurship and innovation to sustain economic growth in an era of global competition and rapid technology advancements. Predictable career paths are challenging in technology companies where product life cycles can be sixty days and employees are all over the world. Demographic trends are driving the need to draw on the talents of a broader group of individuals beyond those who have traditionally launched and led companies. Further, the values and priorities of new workforce entrants may be different than those of their predecessors. It is a complex time for companies and communities that are forced to adapt in real time to these changes, as well as for the academic researchers attempting to study them.

Gender is the overarching topic of these essays. However, trends suggest that research and practice need to be more inclusive of a wider group of individuals with the potential to contribute more fully to entrepreneurship, and to technology fields more generally. It is evident that stereotypes of entrepreneurs and technology leaders continue to favor males, based on their historical participation in these fields and socially constructed gender norms that shape perceptions and assumptions. Further, the portrayal of entrepreneurs as heroes, cowboys, trailblazers, and patriarchs reinforces this, as does the assignment of gender labels such as "masculine" and "feminine" to attributes of entrepreneurs or leaders (Bruni, Gherardi, & Poggio, 2004). Nevertheless, the reality is that females are receiving more undergraduate and graduate degrees than men (National Center for Education Statistics, 2012), and that immigrants, who account for 26 percent of the U.S. population, start businesses at twice the rate of native-born Americans (Fairlie, Morelix, Reedy, & Russell, 2015; Lopez, Passel, & Rohal, 2015). This suggests that if attention and resources are not directed at this broader population, it may result in a significant loss to the economic vibrancy of our communities and nation (Mitchell, 2011).

Much academic research has focused on the gender binary of comparing men and women, as is the case in entrepreneurship, where women and men are often viewed as mutually exclusive groups. An opportunity for future research is more examination of heterogeneity within groups and homogeneity across groups (e.g., gender, generation, cultural background, high- versus low-tech entrepreneurs). To achieve this, study design and the use of metrics other than those associated with high-growth ventures that favor males (e.g., venture capital raised, number of employees) should be used to measure the success and economic impact of a broader population of entrepreneurs (Brush, Carter, Gatewood, Greene, & Hart, 2001; Robb, Coleman, & Stangler, 2014). To cite a case in point, a study by Watson (2002) found that women and men have few performance differences when measured in terms of total income on total assets (as opposed to looking at total income or assets independently), demonstrating that although women wound up with smaller firms, it was because they had fewer assets to begin with and not because there was an inherent difference in their abilities. Alternative measures such as years in business, the ability to support families, and work satisfaction may portray the performance of female and other entrepreneur groups, and their contributions to the economy, in a more positive light.

Themes related to group *identity*, *values*, and *culture* were notable in these essays. Eddleston described women as not identifying with the words "entrepreneur" or "innovation." Swanson spoke to the importance of maintaining the start-up culture to appeal to top technology talent. The descriptions of millennials echoed what in the popular press has been termed the "great generational divide at work" by portraying them to be less interested in promotions and financial rewards than their baby boomer bosses. There are many potential research questions embedded in these observations, and exploring them further could inform practice. For example, research has suggested that media portrayals of millennials may be misleading and, in fact, they may not be much different from other generations (Kowske, Rasch, & Wiley, 2010). While this study may not be conclusive, the example highlights the value of empirical research that examines individual differences within generations, and the effect of contextual (e.g., flatter organizations, job security) or environmental (e.g., historical events, cultural movements) factors on performance, as opposed to labeling groups based on stereotypes or biases.

An overarching question that emerges from chapter 6 is the extent to which educational institutions are preparing graduates for the contemporary workplace. Is the speed of company growth and transformation through acquisitions, mergers, and dissolutions that Swanson described covered in courses? Are conventional human resource paradigms applicable in contexts where employees' roles and responsibilities change every sixty to ninety days? To address these new realities, it is essential that research, teaching, and practice be aligned to optimize company performance and economic growth, and that incentives be in place to achieve this (e.g., research funding, publication outlets). Most importantly, it is essential that our educational programming and pedagogy not reinforce the perception that male entrepreneurs and male technology professionals are the norm.

Given demographic changes and economic realities, it is essential that communities, companies, and educational institutions deploy educational and financial resources in ways that benefit broader populations of individuals. This creates many new opportunities for research related to (a) how to align work policies and practices with new workplace and economic norms; (b) how career success is defined by diverse populations of individuals; and (c) how to motivate people when status and money are not the key drivers of performance.

Managerial and Organizational Actions to Create Inclusive Entrepreneurial Settings

ELLEN ERNST KOSSEK AND KYUNG-HEE LEE

Managerial Actions

- **Develop awareness of prevailing barriers limiting female-led business success, and partner with venture capital firms that support female entrepreneurs.**

Whether you are a women entrepreneur or a manager playing a gatekeeping role in selecting vendors, you should be aware that there is a huge gender gap in funding access and supports for women entrepreneurs. Only 36 percent of small business owners and 9 percent in the technology field are female (Raina, 2016). One of the reasons for this gender gap is funding, and many factors work against female entrepreneurs. First, when venture capital is used for funding, the gender composition of the venture capital firms may influence not only the funding but also the success of the start-up. Research by Raina (2016), based on a large database on technology start-ups, found that not only do female-led start-ups get funded less frequently by venture capital, but they also perform worse than male-led start-ups once funded. Raina attributes these differences to the gender composition of the funding sources because there is no performance difference between female-led and male-led start-ups when the funding venture capital has female partners. His findings suggest that female entrepreneurs select venture capital firms with female partners, which may not be easy in practice. As of 2017, only 8 percent of venture capital partners were female in the United States (Marikar, 2019). However, some female-founded venture capital firms are trying to change the venture capital funding culture by specifically reaching out to female entrepreneurs. For example, Able, founded by two female investors, strives to help female entrepreneurs who lack an elite business school background, as does Female Founders Fund, which only funds female entrepreneurs (Marikar, 2019). Backstage Capital exclusively funds "underestimated" entrepreneurs such as women and LGBTQ individuals (Marikar, 2019).

Researchers Lee & Huang (2018) have found that female-led businesses are also often evaluated as less viable than male-led businesses in general. However, the gender gap decreased when female-led businesses highlighted the social impact of the businesses when pitching for funding, an approach that often resonates with women entrepreneurs' reasons for being in business (Eddleston & Powell, 2008). When social impact is emphasized, not only are investors more likely to be attracted to support women entrepreneurs, but so are customers and employees with growing market power such as millennials. For example, Deloitte (2018) found that millennials list making a positive social impact as one of the top goals for businesses. An example is Hipcamp, a private campground booking site, which found that emphasizing the company's mission of "leaving the environment better than you find it" (Talty, 2018) helped attract new investors and employees.

- **Encourage women employees and suppliers to seek external peer support networks.**
Whether you are a male manager in a big company or a woman employee or entrepreneur, you can play a key role in providing peer support to encourage female entrepreneurs. Networking is very important in professional development, and research suggests that women may need different types of networking support than men do. In a recent study of MBA students, Yang, Chawla, and Uzzi (2019) found that having a small inner-circle network of other women in addition to a wide network with different groups increases women's likelihood of reaching top-level positions, while having an inner circle was not a significant predictor of men's ascent. Similar findings have been reported for female entrepreneurs. In a recent study of female entrepreneurs who participated in Enterprise Ireland female entrepreneur programs (Fullen, 2018), a majority of participants reported that peer support from other female entrepreneurs was very important in helping them grow their businesses by providing practical support (sharing knowledge and exchanging ideas) as well as emotional support (motivating women and providing comfort). In another study (Achor, 2018), women who attended Conferences for Women in several U.S. states were twice as likely to be promoted and three times as likely to get a 10 percent or more pay increase within a year than women who registered but did not attend the conference. Moreover, more than 70 percent of conference attendees reported feeling more optimistic and connected to others than before the conference. An example of another organization that helps women generally, as well as specifically reaching

out to women entrepreneurs to help them find their inner circle, is the Female Quotient (https://thefemalequotient.com), which provides a space for women to gather and network at conferences, corporations, and university campuses. Although restricting support networks only to women has been identified as a risk that can limit women's business potential (Wipp, 2018), overall research shows that having some female peers as a support system is critical to helping women advance in entrepreneurial settings. Managers can encourage and support female employees in entrepreneurial settings and female small-business suppliers to attend gatherings to help grow peer support networks.

Organizational Actions

• **Develop a supplier diversity program to encourage female entrepreneurship.**
Many companies are implementing supplier diversity programs to encourage partnering with entrepreneurs from underrepresented populations such as ethnic minorities, women, LGBTQ individuals, or veterans. These programs benefit not only suppliers but also employers. For example, organizations that spend 20 percent or more of their supply budget on diverse suppliers report 10 percent to 15 percent of their annual sales as a positive return for their investment, while organizations that spend less than 20 percent report less than 5 percent of their annual sales in return (Connaughton & Gibbons, 2016).

Successful supplier diversity programs to support women and minority entrepreneurs have several common attributes. First, their efforts to achieve supplier diversity are tied to core company mission and values. For example, Comcast and NBCUniversal, which were ranked number two by DiversityInc (DiversityInc, n.d.) in 2018, state that their supplier diversity is "core to [their] business continuity" (Kiriacoulacos, n.d.). Second, these programs partner

with organizations that represent entrepreneurs of diverse populations. For example, Accenture, ranked number one by DiversityInc
(DiversityInc, n.d.) in 2018, partners with WEConnect International
(www.weconnectinternational.org), which connects women-owned
businesses with qualified buyers, and Women's Business Enterprise National Council (www.wbenc.org/), which certifies women-
owned businesses to facilitate access to government contracts.
Third, successful programs actively provide resources and invest in
the development of diverse suppliers. Accenture's Diverse Supplier
Development Program is a one-year to one-and-half-year program
through which Accenture's executives become mentors to their
supplier companies, providing education and technical assistance
(Accenture.com, n.d.).

- **Adopt hiring practices that support non-traditional employees
  to help women thrive in entrepreneurial settings.**
Hiring in fast-paced entrepreneurial settings requires innovative
thinking, because the competition for hiring talented people is increasing. Tapping into talent pools of women who are returning
to work can be a good solution that also may increase your firm's
gender diversity (Wells, 2016). Regardless of the reasons for the
break, returning to work after being away from work can be challenging for employees in general, but especially for women who
may have taken time off from work for caregiving. In many entrepreneurial settings where advances in new technologies and other
developments happen fast and often, many returning workers may
feel inadequate to do the job or feel overwhelmed by the gaps in
their knowledge and skills. Returning to work is a bigger issue for
women than men because many women take a break after they have
a baby, whether it is short or long. Moreover, more women than
men serve as day-to-day caregivers for family members, including
children, spouses, and parents (Graf, Brown, & Patten, 2019). Such
commitments mean that, even if they have stayed in the workforce,

women may simply have slowed down their career progress intentionally or because of the dual workload at work and at home.

Employers in general, but especially in entrepreneurial settings, should reach out to skilled women who have been out of work and are interested in working in entrepreneurial settings. One way to do this is to work with organizations that help women with career gaps return to the business labor market. Many for-profit and non-profit organizations connect companies with women who want to return to work. For example, Path Forward (www.pathforward.org), a non-profit organization launched in 2016, works with companies to create a sixteen-week internship program for men and women who want to restart their career after taking a break specifically for caretaking purposes. Their partners include big companies like Walmart, SAP, and NBCUniversal as well as companies in entrepreneurial settings like PayPal, Zendesk, and Udemy. Path Forward reports that 80 percent of women who participated in the program were offered a position from their internship organization, and 90 percent are currently employed (Blumberg, 2017). Another firm, reach IRE (www.reachire.com) focuses exclusively on empowering women who want to return to work. Their internship program is a six-month program with personalized skills training and support.

REFERENCES

Accenture.com. (n.d.). Diversity creates value: Supplier inclusion & sustainability. Retrieved from https://www.accenture.com/us-en/company-supplier-inclusion-diversity.

Achor, S. (2018, 13 February). Do women's networking events move the needle on equality? *Harvard Business Review*. Retrieved from https://hbr.org/2018/02/do-womens-networking-events-move-the-needle-on-equality.

Ahl, H.J. (2002). The making of the female entrepreneur: A discourse analysis of research texts on women's entrepreneurship. (JIBS Dissertation Series No. 015). Jönköping, Sweden: Jönköping University.

Ahl, H. (2006). Why research on women entrepreneurs needs new directions. *Entrepreneurship Theory and Practice, 30*(5), 595–621. https://doi.org/10.1111/j.1540-6520.2006.00138.x

Ahrens, J.P., Landmann, A., & Woywode, M. (2015). Gender preferences in the CEO successions of family firms: Family characteristics and human capital of the successor. *Journal of Family Business Strategy, 6*(2), 86–103. https://doi.org/10.1016/j.jfbs.2015.02.002.

American Express. (2013). State of women-owned businesses report. https://www.americanexpress.com/us/small-business/openforum/keywords/state-of-women-owned-businesses-report/.

Arenius, P., & Autio, E. (2006). Financing of small businesses: Are Mars and Venus more alike than different? *Venture Capital, 8*(02), 93–107. https://doi.org/10.1080/13691060500433793.

BarNir, A., Watson, W.E., & Hutchins, H.M. (2011). Mediation and moderated mediation in the relationship among role models, self-efficacy, entrepreneurial career intention, and gender. *Journal of Applied Social Psychology, 41*(2), 270–97. https://doi.org/10.1111/j.1559-1816.2010.00713.x.

Becker-Blease, J.R., & Sohl, J.E. (2007). Do women-owned businesses have equal access to angel capital? *Journal of Business Venturing, 22*(4), 503–21. https://doi.org/10.1016/j.jbusvent.2006.06.003.

Bird, B., & Brush, C. (2002). A gendered perspective on organizational creation. *Entrepreneurship Theory and Practice, 26*(3), 41–65. https://doi.org/10.1177/104225870202600303.

Bloom, N., & Van Reenen, J. (2007). Measuring and explaining management practices across firms and countries. *The Quarterly Journal of Economics, 122*(4), 1351–1408. https://doi.org/10.1162/qjec.2007.122.4.1351.

Blumberg, M. (2017). Why my startup is betting on "returnships" to help women restart their careers. *Forbes.* Retrieved from https://www.forbes.com/sites/groupthink/2017/04/20/why-my-startup-is-betting-on-returnships-to-help-women-restart-their-careers/.

Bruni, A., Gherardi, S., & Poggio, B. (2004). Entrepreneur-mentality, gender and the study of women entrepreneurs. *Journal of Organizational Change Management*, 17(3), 256–68. https://doi.org/10.1108/09534810410538315.

Brush, C., Carter, N.M., Gatewood, E., Greene, P.G., & Hart, M. (2001). The DIANA Project: Women business owners and equity capital: The myths dispelled. Babson College Center for Entrepreneurship Research Paper No. 2009-11.

Brush, C.G. (1992). Research on women business owners: Past trends, a new perspective and future directions. *Entrepreneurship Theory & Practice*, 16(4), 5–31. https://doi.org/10.1177/104225879201600401.

Carter, N., Brush, C., Greene, P., Gatewood, E., & Hart, M. (2003). Women entrepreneurs who break through to equity financing: The influence of human, social and financial capital. *Venture Capital*, 5(1), 1–28. https://doi.org/10.1080/1369106032000082586.

Carter, N.M., & Williams, M.L. (2003). Comparing social feminism and liberal feminism: The case of new firm growth. In J.E. Butler (Ed.), *New perspectives on women entrepreneurs*, 25–50. Charlotte, NC: Information Age Publishing.

Chaganti, R. (1986). Management in women-owned enterprises. *Journal of Small Business Management*, 24(4), 18–29. https://doi.org/10.1007/978-1-4615-5173-7_7.

Cliff, J.E. (1998). Does one size fit all? Exploring the relationship between attitudes towards growth, gender, and business size. *Journal of Business Venturing*, 13(6), 523–42. https://doi.org/10.1016/S0883-9026(97)00071-2.

Cole, P.M. (1997). Women in family business. *Family Business Review*, 10(4), 353–71. https://doi.org/10.1111/j.1741-6248.1997.00353.x.

Collins-Dodd, C., Gordon, I.M., & Smart, C. (2004). Further evidence on the role of gender in financial performance. *Journal of Small Business Management*, 42(4), 395–417. https://doi.org/10.1111/j.1540-627X.2004.00119.x.

Connaughton, P., & Gibbons, L. (2016). Beyond compliance: Top supplier diversity programs aim to broaden value proposition. *The Hackett*

Group. Retrieved from https://weconnectinternational.org/images
/supplier-inclusion/HackettGroup_SupplierDiversity_2016.pdf.

Cruz, C., Justo, R., & De Castro, J.O. (2012). Does family employment
enhance MSEs performance? Integrating socioemotional wealth and
family embeddedness perspectives. *Journal of Business Venturing, 27*(1),
62–76. https://doi.org/10.1016/j.jbusvent.2010.07.002.

Danes, S.M., Haberman, H.R., & McTavish, D. (2005). Gendered discourse
about family business. *Family Relations, 54*(1), 116–30. https://doi.org
/10.1111/j.0197-6664.2005.00010.x.

Davis, A.E., & Shaver, K.G. (2012). Understanding gendered variations
in business growth intentions across the life course. *Entrepreneurship
Theory and Practice, 36*(3), 495–512. https://doi.org/10.1111/j.1540
-6520.2012.00508.x.

Deloitte. (2018). *Millennial survey 2018*. Retrieved from https://www2
.deloitte.com/global/en/pages/about-deloitte/articles/millennialsurvey
.html.

DeMartino, R., & Barbato, R. (2003). Differences between women and men
MBA entrepreneurs: Exploring family flexibility and wealth creation as
career motivators. *Journal of Business Venturing, 18*(6), 815–32. https://
doi.org/10.1016/S0883-9026(03)00003-X.

DiversityInc. (n.d.). The DiversityInc top companies for supplier
diversity. Retrieved from https://www.diversityinc.com/
diversityinc-top-companies-for-supplier-diversity/.

Dugan, A.M., Krone, S.P., LeCouvie, K., Pendergast, J.M., Kenyon-
Rouvinez, D.H., & Schuman, A.M. (2011). *A woman's place: The crucial
roles of women in family business*. Marietta, GA: Family Business
Consulting Group.

Economist, The. (2006, 15 April). The importance of sex. Retrieved from
http://www.economist.com/node/6800723.

Eddleston, K.A., Ladge, J.J., Mitteness, C., & Balachandra, L. (2016). Do
you see what I see? Signaling effects of gender and firm characteristics
on financing entrepreneurial ventures. *Entrepreneurship Theory and
Practice, 40*(3), 489–514. https://doi.org/10.1111/etap.12117.

Eddleston, K.A., & Powell, G.N. (2008). The role of gender identity in explaining sex differences in business owners' career satisfier preferences. *Journal of Business Venturing*, 23(2), 244–56. https://doi.org/10.1016/j.jbusvent.2006.11.002.

Eddleston, K.A., & Powell, G.N. (2012). Nurturing entrepreneurs' work–family balance: A gendered perspective. *Entrepreneurship Theory and Practice*, 36(3), 513–41. https://doi.org/10.1111/j.1540-6520.2012.00506.x.

EY Report. (2015). Women in leadership: The family business advantage. Retrieved from http://www.ey.com/GL/en/Services/Strategic-Growth-Markets/Family-business/ey-women-in-leadership-the-family-business-advantage.

Fairlie, R.W., Morelix, A., Reedy, E.J., & Russell, J. (2015). The Kauffman index 2015: Startup activity: National trends. Kauffman Foundation. Retrieved from https://www.kauffman.org/~/media/kauffman_org/research%20reports%20and%20covers/2015/05/kauffman_index_startup_activity_national_trends_2015.pdf.

Fairlie, R.W., & Robb, A.M. (2009). Gender differences in business performance: Evidence from the Characteristics of Business Owners survey. *Small Business Economics*, 33(4), 375–95. https://doi.org/10.1007/s11187-009-9207-5.

Freudenberger, H.J., Freedheim, D.K., Kurtz, T.S., & Kurtz, T.S. (1989). Treatment of individuals in family businesses. *Psychotherapy: Theory, Research, Practice, Training*, 26(1), 47–53. https://doi.org/10.1037/h0085404.

Fullen, H. (2018). *The value of peer support in female business venturing*. Retrieved from https://issuu.com/helenfullen/docs/_the_value_of_peer_support_in_femal/1.

GEM (Global Entrepreneurship Monitor). (2013). 2012 global report. Retrieved from https://gemconsortium.org/report/gem-2012-global-report.

Goffee, R., & Scase, R. (1985). *Women in charge: The experiences of female entrepreneurs*. London: Allen & Unwin.

Graf, N., Brown, A., & Patten, E. (2019, 22 March). The narrowing, but persistent, gender gap in pay. *Pew Research Center*. Retrieved from

https://www.pewresearch.org/fact-tank/2019/03/22/gender-pay
-gap-facts/.

Gupta, V.K., Turban, D.B., & Pareek, A. (2013). Differences between
men and women in opportunity evaluation as a function of gender
stereotypes and stereotype activation. *Entrepreneurship Theory and
Practice*, 37(4), 771–88. https://doi.org/10.1111/j.1540-6520.2012.00512.x.

Gupta, V.K., Turban, D.B., Wasti, S.A., & Sikdar, A. (2009). The role of
gender stereotypes in perceptions of entrepreneurs and intentions to
become an entrepreneur. *Entrepreneurship Theory and Practice*, 33(2),
397–417. https://doi.org/10.1111/j.1540-6520.2009.00296.x.

Harrison, J.D. (2015). The decline of American entrepreneurship – in
five charts. *The Washington Post*. Retrieved from https://www
.washingtonpost.com/news/on-small-business/wp/2015/02/12
/the-decline-of-american-entrepreneurship-in-five-charts/.

Hughes, K.D., Jennings, J.E., Brush, C., Carter, S., & Welter, F. (2012).
Extending women's entrepreneurship research in new directions.
Entrepreneurship Theory and Practice, 36(3), 429–42. https://doi
.org/10.1111/j.1540-6520.2012.00504.x.

Jennings, J.E., & Brush, C.G. (2013). Research on women entrepreneurs:
Challenges to (and from) the broader entrepreneurship literature? *The
Academy of Management Annals*, 7(1), 663–715. https://doi.org/10.1080
/19416520.2013.782190.

Jennings, J.E., & McDougald, M.S. (2007). Work-family interface
experiences and coping strategies: Implications for entrepreneurship
research and practice. *Academy of Management Review*, 32(3), 747–60.
https://doi.org/10.1080/19416520.2013.782190.

Jimenez, R. (2009). Research on women in family firms: Current status and
future directions. *Family Business Review*, 22(1), 53–64. https://doi.org
/10.1177/0894486508328813.

Kauffman Foundation. (2015). *State of entrepreneurship: Mixed indicators
prompt call for entrepreneurial renewal*. Retrieved from http://www
.kauffman.org/newsroom/2015/02/state-of-entrepreneurship-mixed
-indicators-prompt-call-for-entrepreneurial-renewal.

Kelley, D.J., Brush, C.G., Greene, P.G., & Litovsky, Y. (2011). *Global entrepreneurship monitor; 2010 women's report.* Babson Park, MA: Babson College, Global Entrepreneurship Research Association. Retrieved from https://cdn.ymaws.com/www.andeglobal.org/resource/dynamic /blogs/20111215_125335_17430.pdf.

Kiriacoulacos, P. (n.d.). Supplier diversity: Core to our business continuity. Retrieved from https://corporate.comcast.com/news-information /news-feed/supplier-diversity-core.

Kowske, B.J., Rasch, R., & Wiley, J. (2010). Millennials' (lack of) attitude problem: An empirical examination of generational effects on work attitudes. *Journal of Business and Psychology*, *25*(2), 265–79. https://doi .org/10.1007/s10869-010-9171-8.

Lee, M., & Huang, L. (2018). Gender bias, social impact framing, and evaluation of entrepreneurial ventures. *Organization Science*, *29*(1), 1–16. https://doi.org/10.1287/orsc.2017.1172.

Lopez, M.H., Passel, J., & Rohal, M. (2015). Modern immigration wave brings 59 million to US, driving population growth and change through 2065. *Pew Research Center.* Retrieved from https://www.pewresearch .org/hispanic/wp-content/uploads/sites/5/2015/09/2015-09-28 _modern-immigration-wave_REPORT.pdf.

Loscocco, K., & Bird, S.R. (2012). Gendered paths: Why women lag behind men in small business success. *Work and Occupations*, *39*(2), 183–219. https://doi.org/10.1177/0730888412444282.

Loscocco, K., & Smith-Hunter, A. (2004). Women home-based business owners: Insights from comparative analyses. *Women in Management Review*, *19*(3), 164–73. https://doi.org/10.1108/09649420410529870.

Loscocco, K.A., Robinson, J., Hall, R.H., & Allen, J.K. (1991). Gender and small business success: An inquiry into women's relative disadvantage. *Social Forces*, *70*(1), 65–85. https://doi.org/10.2307/2580062.

MacNeil, N. 2012. Entrepreneurship is the new women's movement. *Forbes.* Retrieved from http://www.forbes.com/sites/work-in -progress/2012/06/08/entrepreneurship-is-the-new-womens -movement/#3beb20066922.

Marikar, S. (2019, 5 March). When women control the money, female
   founders get funded. *The New York Times*. Retrieved from https://www
   .nytimes.com/2019/03/01/business/female-founders-venture-capital
   .html.

Mass Mutual. (2007). American family business survey. Retrieved from
   https://www.massmutual.com/mmfg/pdf/afbs.pdf.

Menzies, T.V., Diochon, M., & Gasse, Y. (2004). Examining venture-related
   myths concerning women entrepreneurs. *Journal of Developmental
   Entrepreneurship, 9*(2), 89–107. Retrieved from https://search.proquest
   .com/docview/208428310?accountid=13360.

Mitchell, L. (2011). Overcoming the gender gap: Women entrepreneurs
   as economic drivers. Kauffman Foundation. Retrieved from https://
   www.kauffman.org/~/media/kauffman_org/research%20reports
   %20and%20covers/2011/09/growing_the_economy_women
   _entrepreneurs.pdf.

Morris, M.H., Miyasaki, N.N., Watters, C.E., & Coombes, S.M. (2006). The
   dilemma of growth: Understanding venture size choices of women
   entrepreneurs. *Journal of Small Business Management, 44*(2), 221–44.
   https://doi.org/10.1111/j.1540-627X.2006.00165.x.

National Center for Education Statistics. (2012). *The condition of education.*
   Retrieved from https://nces.ed.gov/pubsearch/pubsinfo.asp?pubid
   =2012045.

Nelton, S. (1998). The rise of women in family firms: A call for research
   now. *Family Business Review, 11*(3), 215–18. https://doi.org/10.1111
   /j.1741-6248.1998.00215.x.

Powell, G.N. (2011). The gender and leadership wars. *Organizational
   Dynamics, 40*(1), 1–9. https://doi.org/10.1016/j.orgdyn.2010.10.009.

Powell, G.N., & Eddleston, K.A. (2008). The paradox of the contented
   female business owner. *Journal of Vocational Behavior, 73*(1), 24–36.
   https://doi.org/10.1016/j.jvb.2007.12.005.

Powell, G.N., & Eddleston, K.A. (2013). Linking family-to-business
   enrichment and support to entrepreneurial success: Do female and
   male entrepreneurs experience different outcomes? *Journal of Business
   Venturing, 28*(2), 261–80. https://doi.org/10.1016/j.jbusvent.2012.02.007.

Raina, S. (2016, 19 July). Research: The gender gap in startup success
disappears when women fund women. *Harvard Business Review.*
Retrieved from https://hbr.org/2016/07/research-the-gender-gap-in
-startup-success-disappears-when-women-fund-women.

Robb, A., Coleman, S., & Stangler, D. (2014). Sources of economic
hope: Women's entrepreneurship. Retrieved from http://www
.kauffman.org/~/media/kauffman_org/research%20reports%20
and%20covers/2014/11/sources_of_economic_hope_womens
_entrepreneurship.pdf.

Robb, A.M., & Watson, J. (2012). Gender differences in firm performance:
Evidence from new ventures in the United States. *Journal of Business
Venturing, 27*(5), 544–58. https://doi.org/10.1016/j.jbusvent.2011.10.002.

Rowe, B.R., & Hong, G.S. (2000). The role of wives in family businesses:
The paid and unpaid work of women. *Family Business Review, 13*(1),
1–13. https://doi.org/10.1111/j.1741-6248.2000.00001.x.

Salganicoff, M. (1990). Women in family businesses: Challenges and
opportunities. *Family Business Review, 3*(2), 125–37. https://doi
.org/10.1111/j.1741-6248.1990.00125.x.

Schumpeter, J.A. (1934). *The theory of economic development: An inquiry
into profits, capital, credit, interest, and the business cycle.* Vol. 55. New
Brunswick, NJ, and London: Transaction publishers.

Shelton, L.M. (2006). Female entrepreneurs, work-family conflict, and
venture performance: New insights into the work-family interface.
Journal of Small Business Management, 44(2), 285–97. https://doi
.org/10.1111/j.1540-627X.2006.00168.x.

Sullivan, D.M., & Meek, W.R. (2012). Gender and entrepreneurship: A
review and process model. *Journal of Managerial Psychology, 27*(5), 428–58.
https://doi.org/10.1108/02683941211235373.

Talty, A. (2018). How 29-year-old CEO Alyssa Ravasio is changing
American camping. *Forbes.* Retrieved from https://www.forbes.com
/sites/alexandratalty/2018/04/30/how-29-year-old-ceo-alyssa
-ravasio-is-changing-american-camping/.

Watson, J. (2002). Comparing the performance of male- and female-
controlled businesses: Relating outputs to inputs. *Entrepreneurship:*

Theory and Practice, 26(3), 91–101. https://doi.org/10.1177 /104225870202600306.

Watson, J., & Robinson, S. (2003). Adjusting for risk in comparing the performances of male- and female-controlled SMEs. *Journal of Business Venturing, 18*(6), 773–88. https://doi.org/10.1016/S0883 -9026(02)00128-3.

Wells, G. (2016, 10 April). Tech companies help women get back to work. *Wall Street Journal*. Retrieved from https://www.wsj.com/articles /tech-companies-help-women-get-back-to-work-1460309159.

Wilson, F., Kickul, J., & Marlino, D. (2007). Gender, entrepreneurial self-efficacy, and entrepreneurial career intentions: Implications for entrepreneurship education. *Entrepreneurship Theory and Practice, 31*(3), 387–406. https://doi.org/10.1111/j.1540-6520.2007.00179.x.

Wipp, N. (2018, 14 September). Female entrepreneurs: If you're networking mostly with women, you're leaving money on the table. *Entrepreneur*. Retrieved from https://www.entrepreneur.com /article/319117.

Wu, Z., & Chua, J.H. (2012). Second-order gender effects: The case of US small business borrowing cost. *Entrepreneurship Theory and Practice, 36*(3), 443–63. https://doi.org/10.1111/j.1540-6520.2012.00503.x.

Yang, Y., Chawla, N.V., & Uzzi, B. (2019). A network's gender composition and communication pattern predict women's leadership success. *Proceedings of the National Academy of Sciences, 116*(6), 2033–8. https:// doi.org/10.1073/pnas.1721438116.

Zarya, V. (2015, 21 August). The fastest-growing group of entrepreneurs in the U.S.? Minority women. *Fortune*. Retrieved from http://fortune .com/2015/08/21/women-small-business-diverse/.

7

EPILOGUE: A BEGINNING BLUEPRINT FOR ORGANIZATIONS AND RESEARCHERS TO ADVANCE GENDER INCLUSION AND EQUALITY (WITH CAVEATS)

ELLEN ERNST KOSSEK AND KYUNG-HEE LEE

If you want to change the culture, you will have to start by changing the organization.

– Mary Douglas, British anthropologist

Each chapter in this book provides evidence suggesting that persistent challenges remain in enhancing gender inclusion and fostering women's representation in leadership positions in business and society to close the gender gap. Taken together, we identified the following overarching themes.

Key Chapter Themes Recap

First, there is a need to improve practitioner (and scholarly) understanding of core concepts related to diversity and gender inclusion (D&I) (Nishii, chapter 2). There is a lack of clarity about (1) what the differences are between diversity and inclusion (Roberson, 2006); (2) what are the antecedents and conditions that foster gender inclusion; and (3) how to measure it (Shore,

Cleveland, & Sanchez, 2018). Such a lack of clarity in practice and among scholars may be holding back workplace D&I innovation and scholarly advancement of knowledge. Most importantly, we need to broaden research from largely focusing on describing what is wrong with organizations to investigating how to create change toward positive gender-inclusive environments. Such an approach will move the diversity and inclusion conversation from "leaving conversations" to "staying conversations," as Accenture's Nellie Borrero aptly stated.

Second, our knowledge of how to challenge prevailing barriers to move the gender inclusion needle in organizations is still insufficient. Take mentoring, for example, which has been researched for decades. There is still some conflicting dialogue in the D&I community about how to definitively break glass ceilings through implementing quality mentoring (Ragins, chapter 3). We need to increase the literacy of scholars and the workforce about the pros and cons of different types of mentoring (e.g., formal and informal; cross-gender versus same-gender) and the attributes of quality design in mentoring initiatives. We need to advance the science of diversity initiatives from mentoring to talent management programs to be more evidence-based and scientifically clear about what works, under what conditions, and for whom.

Third, work teams are the essential building block for positively moving the corporate culture toward greater inclusion, assuming that steps are taken to reduce stereotyping and biases (Loyd, chapter 4). Targeting change initiatives at this level can be a powerful lever for workplace change. As PwC's Anne Donovan observes, generational diversity is likely to increase in the workplace. Managing the intersectionality between age and gender diversity may be increasingly critical and could adversely impact women. For example, many women may advance to senior career stages more slowly than their male counterparts, particularly if they have had to juggle family needs early in their careers or manage elder and spouse care later on in sandwiched years. Yet evidence is growing that many women experience a burst of creativity and are able to produce additional high value contributions to the organization about five to ten years later than their male counterparts of similar age (Goldin & Katz, 2018). Actions must be taken to ensure senior and mid-level women are not overlooked for high potential lists or talent development if they are older than their similarly positioned male counterparts. More research and interventions are clearly needed on these possible gendered age diversity impacts on how to enhance opportunities and remove barriers to women's career equality.

Fourth, gender inclusion occurs in specific job, workgroup, and organizational and occupational contexts. Obstacles and initiatives must be understood and customized accordingly. For example, leaders seeking to advance women in STEM contexts need not only to actively increase the pipeline of female talent but also to look at the intersectionality of gender and race to deal with specific inclusion challenges in disciplinary and workplace environments. For instance, a recent study of women in astronomy found that women of color report the highest rates of harassment compared to other women (Clancy, Lee, Rodgers, & Richey, 2017). And such dynamics may be heightened when women are more severely underrepresented in a particular discipline. For example, while women represent only 17 percent of computer science majors, they make up 40 percent of math majors (Bach, 2016). STEM cultures that were experienced as higher on masculinity tended to have disciplinary stereotypes that were incongruent with how many women perceived their identities, non-positive stereotypes about women's abilities, and few female role models (Bach, 2016). Besides disciplinary and organizational culture, managers and scholars must consider the impact of national culture values toward women in a particular society, as many foreign-born women are working in cross-national STEM contexts (Mack, Sahley, & Taylor, chapter 5).

Fifth, entrepreneurial and internet settings are often so fast-paced, with very short-term employment expectations, that it may be more difficult to take the time to develop long-term relational-based cultures that may be helpful to the inclusion of women. In addition, wide legal differences exist around the globe, such as the ability of women to own property, go to school, or work outside the home without their husband's or a male relative's permission. It is important to be aware of such differences across country contexts in order to understand the institutionalized national structural and cultural barriers to women's advancement (Eddleston, chapter 6).

Avoiding the Hype and the Knowing-Doing Gap

Even when organizational leaders and researchers understand the state of the science, there can be a common tripwire that Stanford Business School professors Jeff Pfeffer and Bob Sutton (2000) refer to as a "knowing-doing gap." This refers to the fact that organizations, leaders, and scholars can cognitively understand the current state-of-the-art inclusion science and best research evidence and practices yet fail to implement these ideas in practice and change efforts. Despite the current heightened attention to diversity and inclusion, and the millions of dollars organizations spend to pay consultants – both internal and external – on diversity efforts, *the sad reality is that most diversity efforts fail to produce diversity* (Dobbin & Kalev, 2016). Despite the hype around the globe on the importance of advancing gender inclusion, and related growing government and corporate lip service, progress remains slow across and at the highest levels of society. In the United States, for example, there has never been a woman president or even vice-president elected in its history. As of this book's publishing, there remains a lack of public paid maternity or paternity leave – the United States is one of the few countries that lack such policies out of a handful of industrialized nations (Kossek, 2019). Fewer than 5 percent of CEOs are women (Mejia, 2018). As one of the editors of this book stated as a participant on a panel on women's career equality that opened the conference that provided much of the content for this book,

> I just hope that this attention to gender and inclusion diversity is not a fad. When I was in grad school (I studied) ... human resource innovation

... the HERWEGA effect, the "here we go again effect." This concept was mentioned to me by an advisor, Dr Clay Alderfer (now deceased), when I was a doctoral student at Yale School of Management. Companies are ... very faddish, and a lot of things that we're talking about now, I was studying (back) in grad school (several decades ago). (Kossek, 2016)

To avoid this pattern of cycles of promoting and starting to attempt diversity initiatives but then not really implementing them and moving on to the next "flavor of the month," let's take a look toward the future to identify key themes regarding how to begin to build a gender-inclusive climate for women.

A Blueprint for Advancing Gender Inclusion (with a Few Caveats)

If you are an organizational leader or an employee reading this book, you can consider whether and how effectively your workplace is implementing any of the following recommended actions. If you are a scholar, student, or consultant, you can assess how to advance science and practice to make inclusive practices more widespread across employing organizations. However, in order not to give the impression that advancing gender and diversity is easy, or that the state of evidence-based science provides a clear blueprint, for each theme we suggest caveats such as possible unintended consequences to watch out for or, where appropriate, unanswered or under-investigated research questions.

- **Attend to and integrate multilevel metrics and systemic approaches when diagnosing and measuring women's career equality.**
Advancing gender inclusion and equality requires all of us to seek evidence-based understanding of how women across the spectrum of job and social identity groups vary in experiencing the workplace

in terms of their psychological experiences and career outcomes, and to identify conditions and requisite integrative solutions to foster women's career success (Novotney, 2019) and equality. Doing so may require a holistic approach to developing metrics to study and measure career equality across various levels of analysis, and perspectives on why women haven't advanced. Often many organizations find it appealing to focus on individual indicators and self-improvement activities, such as telling women just to take more prescribed STEM or business classes, be more confident, find a mentor, or simply "lean in" as a path toward greater inclusion and equity. Yet we believe that individual metrics and solutions as an isolated strategy may overly focus on "fixing individual women" to increase their skills and abilities. Such an approach will not necessarily diagnose group or organizational barriers that prevent the creation of more gender-inclusive workplaces that advance women's career equality.

Making metrics matter: the need for multilevel multifaceted metrics. We believe that inclusion and equality metrics need to be customized to fit the job demands for each industry and simultaneously include initiatives targeting at least two levels of change to enable us to understand how societal, organizational, and group dynamics related to women's gender and career inclusion shape individual experiences as a "nested social phenomenon." For example, women in organizations that have gender-balanced representation at the top are likely to have more positive and less competitive gender relations among women peers at lower levels of the firm, as the culture is less likely to foster negative competitive gender dynamics as token hires battle to advance (Ely, 1994). Besides not just measuring progress at one level or in one activity, Kossek and colleagues (Kossek, Su, & Wu, 2017) argue that it is important to integrate disciplinary narratives (career preference, gender bias, work-family, among others) on career equality barriers and metrics involving linked solutions addressing why women are not advancing at similar rates to men. For example, "downstream" metrics on the number of college women selecting and staying in STEM majors should also examine the "upstream" societal metrics of whether sufficient resources are being devoted to developing a pipeline of young women who are learning about STEM at an early age (addressing career interests and socialization metrics). Such metrics might also assess the number of young women having the experience to hold leadership positions while in school, and having access to role models (bias-related metrics).

Similarly, metrics on the representation of women on boards of directors should not just measure the number of women on boards, addressing gender career equity in representation, but also the number of women on boards who have been able to care for children and raise a family in a gender-egalitarian household (addressing work-life inequality metrics as well). Such multifaceted metrics are needed to ensure that women board members have similar work-life and career experiences to those of their male board member counterparts. Although such multifaceted approaches ideally should be considered simultaneously when organizations develop new policies, programs, or interventions, or when researchers design related studies, we argue that one of the barriers to implementing successful gender inclusion initiatives is that organizations and researchers rarely effectively link multidisciplinary views to address the different reasons *why* women are not advancing in organizations. Below we will illustrate the implications for intervention design and caveats if only one perspective is considered.

- **To avoid unintended consequences of isolated content strategies, avoid over-focusing on one narrative in designing interventions.** Organizations and researchers often prefer to focus on one narrative and over-simplify the solutions for inclusion. In this section, we will review three common explanations (cf Kossek et al., 2017) on how to foster women's inclusion – address women's career preferences, gender bias, and work-family inequality experiences – and then consider the caveats of implementing each as an isolated strategy.

Career preference attraction and recruitment as a singular strategy. The career preference narrative attributes gendered career paths such as having lower women's representation hierarchically and functionally to glass ceilings in tech or manufacturing; or over-representation in "softer areas" such as human resources rather than in "hard science areas" such as engineering, for example, to a lack of person-environment fit between the work environment and women's interests, values, and needs (Diekman, Brown, Johnston, & Clark, 2010). Based on this narrative, jobs should be redesigned to be better suited for women's interests, values, and goals, ensuring that women will experience more positive career outcomes and performance (Nye, Su, Rounds, & Drasgow, 2012). For example, when recruiting women to work in tech, companies are more likely to attract women by publicizing that they are hiring applicants who "desire to advance society's sustainability" than if they are stating that they are seeking "aggressive rock stars" (Eddleston & Powell, 2008).

Possible caveats against mainly focusing interventions to target career preferences. If recruitment strategies are only redesigned to fit career preferences without also attending to negative gender-bias dynamics in the job context, such efforts could backfire once women are hired, and turnover may ensue. Even if the firm is more successful in attracting and hiring women to work in non-traditional roles in a high tech firm, these women may not experience the culture as supportive of their needs and values. Individual women are likely to face personal backlash if the internal culture does not match the recruitment message that women are valued and their cultural values are supported.

Simultaneous strategies to reduce gender-stereotyping of women leaders and possible discrimination for being a token hire may be needed as well. For example, increasing workplace empathy training through role plays that focus on women's career experiences and improve listening skills can help reduce gender bias in organizations and create a gender-inclusive climate. Several studies (Batson, Polycarpou, Harmon-Jones, et al., 1997; Burke et al., 2015; Todd, Bodenhausen, Richeson, & Galinsky, 2011) identified empathy as a key mechanism to reduce biases against various identity groups (including women). Many organizations have been implementing empathy training for their employees and managers because empathy is related to improvement in collaboration and morale (Zaki,

2019) as well as to companies' bottom line. In 2015, the income per employee in the top ten organizations in Global Empathy Index was 50 percent more than that in the bottom ten organizations (Lubin, 2016). Future research and practice need to identify more ways to jointly enhance women's person-environment-career fit in work contexts where they are underrepresented and evaluate the effectiveness of improved recruitment, training, and other bias-busting activities that support women's retention.

Training on gender bias as a singular strategy. The gender-bias narrative (Eagly & Karau, 2002) argues that women are held back in their careers because of the persistence of objective and subjective barriers and bias that exclude them from leadership positions. Based on gender roles in society, when women act in ways that are not in line with traditional role expectations, such as being nurturing and assertive, they face backlash and negative career outcomes (Diekman & Eagly, 2008). Organizations need to educate and train their employees on how to manage gender bias. The empathy training to address bias described above is one example.

Possible caveats against only focusing on raising awareness via gender-bias training. While bias training can increase members' knowledge and awareness of gender bias, simply training people on their biases may not necessarily foster cultural change to reduce bias and increase support of women's career and work-life needs. Bias training that focuses on negative incentives or messages (e.g., "not hiring enough women hurts the company image and bottom line") does not get lasting results, and the mandatory nature of the training can evoke participant resistance (Dobbin & Kalev, 2016). In fact, some scholars argue that it can backfire and may condone stereotyping (Duguid & Thomas-Hunt, 2015) if there are no positive incentives to engage in less bias on the job tied to improvement in meeting organizational diversity goals (Zhao, 2019) and transferring the training behaviors on bias into everyday interactions. The training needs to include practical workplace examples and specific actions employees can take to improve bias management in everyday interactions (Emerson, 2017). Moreover, training needs to caution members that even though *some* women may prefer to act in ways that are aligned with traditional gender roles (e.g., being nurturing, showing communal values), not *all* women may act this way. All members of a common gender group may not act in line with traditional gender-role expectations.

Addressing work-family support needs as a singular strategy. Some companies may focus on work-family support as a way to address the fact that many women face inclusion and career-equality barriers due to gender differences in work and family dynamics. Central to this perspective is the growth of single-parent and dual-career families where many women are still managing more of the non-work demands, as well as experiencing stigma if they work fewer visible face-time hours or use workplace flexibility (e.g., telework, part-time work, flextime) to a greater extent than their male counterparts (Kossek, 2006). Although family/life-friendly policies such as flexible work-family arrangements and parental leaves for both men and women have the potential to advance gender inclusion, they often fall short in implementation.

Possible caveats against only focusing on work-family support. When companies offer work and family programs but do not address the stigma of using them, or when career assumptions are made about women who equally value their family and work, individuals (often women) who are heavier users of work-family supports will be marginalized and face overwork stress, and masculinity-oriented organizational cultures will prevail. As a study drawing on fifteen years of data found (Park, Lee, & Budd, 2019), using paid maternity leave decreased women's wage growth by 3.1 percent. Also, working women who also have primary responsibility for caring for children may be using flexibility in different ways than their male counterparts. These women may be multitasking to manage both work and childcare demands, which increases overload and process losses from intense simultaneous dual role enactment.

Conclusion. We argue that interventions and strategies often do not link multiple barriers to women's lack of advancement effectively, which may limit the effectiveness of workplace actions. We recommend that researchers and workplaces assess multiple cultural reasons why women are not advancing or experiencing the workplace positively and develop integrative solutions relying on several inclusion frameworks and remedies simultaneously.

- **Implement initiatives that target change to improve the context in which individual and group women's inclusion and career-equality experiences are situated.**

We've noted the importance of understanding that individual career experiences of women are often embedded in and influenced by the dynamics of a woman's workgroup, team, occupation, organization, and society. Thus, individual experiences are often linked to influences from higher-level contexts that we often overlook. Consequently, researchers and change agents need to consider how the concepts of gender inclusion – such as ensuring fairness and non-discrimination, leveraging talent, and supporting women's values, interests, and needs (and voice) to foster belongingness – involve individual, workgroup, and organizational processes in the design and implementation of initiatives. For example, if individual women experience discrimination, it is likely that this is because the company's equal-opportunity policies related to selection, performance appraisal, or pay practices are not enforced, communicated, or implemented well either in their work unit or across the firm. To remedy this, during performance appraisal, a firm might evaluate first-line managers on their actions to support HR policies relevant to gender equality and inclusion (Babcock, 2009; Zhao, 2019) at the same time that they review all the policies at the organizational level for adverse impact, and implement ways to improve related selection and performance evaluation policies to remove criteria that are not validated as job-related (Mackenzie, Wehner, & Correll, 2019).

- **Encourage collaboration between researchers and organizations to advance gender inclusion and career equality, and, where possible, conduct group-randomized control or quasi-experimental field experiments.**

Perhaps one of the most important ways to advance gender inclusion and diversity in organizations is through ongoing researcher and practitioner partnerships to design and evaluate evidence-based field experiments. Indeed, studies show that one of the best ways to address gender-equality gaps is to seek progress through organization and research collaboration (PwC, 2013). When organizations invite researchers to their organization either to understand the current status of the organization or to solve problems, the results are enlightening, promising, and impactful. These partnerships should be conducted based on scientific field methods – such as, when possible, using a randomized control study with a control group to evaluate the effects of following usual practice versus implementing the inclusion intervention. A wait-list control design also offers a way to gradually introduce new D&I initiatives by offering the practice later to the control group, while allowing researchers the capability to compare the control and intervention groups and evaluate the effectiveness of the initiatives. Naturally occurring quasi-experiments offer another opportunity for learning. For example, perhaps the Australian division of a global firm is implementing new policies to meet a law on the right to request a flexible schedule. The company could compare turnover rates pre- and post-implementation or compare the results in Australia to a similar sample of employees in another country that does not offer a right to request flexibility.

When researchers can implement rigorous investigations on new company or societal initiatives and interventions, the findings can be more widely adapted, disseminated, and replicated in other organizations and societies. Researcher-employer collaboration enables scientific testing of theories and interventions, as well as fine-tuning and customization to fit the needs of society and organizations generally.

Possible caveats against researcher-organizational collaboration. Although it is clear that researchers and organizations can benefit much from ongoing collaboration, just the mere act of collaboration may not necessarily advance successful gender inclusion. For example, an organization may back out of the partnership if the organization doesn't allow the researchers to feed back the data in ways that reduce survey fatigue from many research studies and show how the research is personally beneficial (Bilimoria, 2019). Moreover, conflicts between researchers and organizations may arise when the results researchers find are not favorable to the organization (Ankrah & AL-Tabbaa, 2015), or when researchers find something they are obligated to report, such as discrimination. To avoid conflicts, reaching a formal agreement regarding the goals of the project and what each party is expected to do during the collaboration is important for successful collaboration (Ankrah & AL-Tabbaa, 2015). The agreement may include discussions about how parties could resolve possible conflicts (Amabile et al., 2001). For example, researchers can assure the organization that the identity of the organization will be confidential and the results will be presented with a pseudonym. Researchers can also inform organizations in advance about situations that researchers are ethically and legally obligated to report to authority, such as sexual abuse or gender or racial discrimination. Clarifying goals, expectations, and processes at the beginning of the collaboration will increase the likelihood that the collaboration is a success.

- **Actively increase women's access to mentoring, peer support, and formal and informal networks.**
Research shows that peer support and support from sponsors with power are critical to women's inclusion and advancement and that these mentoring initiatives must be of high quality. High-quality mentoring programs start with needs and readiness assessment (Allen, Finkelstein, & Poteet, 2009). Because each organization has different mentoring challenges related to inclusion, it is important to

conduct a cultural diagnosis of how to tailor a firm's mentoring program to the organization's specific needs before adopting or refining programs. This will help employers to more effectively establish objectives, target participants, and identify the resources needed to build a successful mentoring program. To ensure that mentors and protégés build quality relationships, successful mentoring programs need protocols for training, monitoring, and the evaluation of processes – ideally by outside researchers partnering with internal leaders (Allen et al., 2009).

Possible caveats. Despite mounting research evidence and evidence from many successful organizational mentoring programs, women still face challenges in receiving good mentoring, and implementing effective, high-quality mentoring programs is difficult. Such challenges have only increased in the #MeToo era. Organizations that implement mentoring programs also need to invest in educating and training their mentors and mentees to ensure that they feel safe and comfortable in the relationships and that mentoring initiatives do not stall. Such training may not only reduce the potential for sexual harassment but also enhance relational quality because the quality of the mentoring relationship is important in successful mentoring initiatives. Besides formal mentoring relationships, women professionals need organizational support in cultivating peer support systems – often consisting of other women. These peer inner circles can provide practical as well as emotional support to help women navigate often male-dominated professional life. Yet some companies may find it difficult to simultaneously implement both women-focused and organizational- and mentor-focused change.

Moreover, while mentoring is critical for women's advancement, some companies may implement their mentoring program in a way that focuses all the attention on addressing women's skill gaps and increasing social support rather than on actually changing the culture and structure to eliminate institutional biases. Some critics now advocate not just for women's mentoring but for increasing women's sponsorship where a senior manager advocates for a women's advancement. They argue that while mentoring focuses on providing teaching, feedback, and advice, sponsorship actively advocates for the protégé using the sponsor's influence (Helms, Arfken, & Bellar, 2016). Regardless of the term used, mentoring, when used as an isolated strategy, is a necessary but insufficient condition to ensure women's career advancement. For example, a meta-analysis study on the organizational contextual conditions that foster the effectiveness of women's mentoring initiatives (Ghosh, 2014) found that organizational support for mentoring is important in successful mentoring programs. Organizational support for mentoring means that mentoring participants believe that "agents in the organization recognize the importance of mentoring, that managerial role models for appropriate mentoring are available, and that mentors are rewarded for their mentoring efforts" (Eby, Lockwood, & Butts, 2006, 270). However, the study also found that organizational support for mentoring is highest at the early phase of the mentoring program but slowly decreases with the progression of the phases (Ghosh, 2014). For optimal results, organizations need to maintain a consistent level of support for their mentoring program throughout the various phases of the program.

- **Develop a strong public commitment (backed up with internal data) by the firm's senior organizational leaders to create a gender-inclusive culture.**

Messaging and commitment from top management are critical first steps toward increasing the inclusion and advancement of women in organizations and closing the gender gap. Employers and organizational members need to begin by developing a common understanding of key indicators of a strong gender-inclusive climate. For example, to what extent do members feel that the workplace climate values and supports women's talents for leadership roles? To what extent do women feel that they do not have to sacrifice core aspects of their identities (such as mother, spouse) in order to advance? To what extent are women able to speak up about implicit and explicit discrimination without retribution (Kossek et al., 2017)? Are there men as strong allies who will also actively speak up on these issues to support women and ensure that women who speak up about bias do not face discrimination (Novotney, 2019)?

In order to create such a climate, one key action is having a leader, such as a chief executive officer (CEO), speak out and pledge their commitment to advancing diversity and inclusion. Created in 2017, CEO Action Pledge for Diversity and Inclusion (www.ceoaction. com) now has more than 650 CEOs around the world who are pledged to improve workplace diversity and inclusion. Many CEOs are openly voicing their support for advancing women's and minorities' careers and improving workplace experiences. For example, as the CEO of Salesforce recently stated, "Diversity is an important part of our culture of equality. Our employees are telling us that they want to work for a company that cares about diversity, and it helps us recruit people whose values align to ours" (Johnson, 2017).

Possible caveats. Sometimes companies can publicize and adopt diversity initiatives as public relations actions or administrative vehicles that conceal discrimination within the firm (Konrad & Linnehan, 1995). Firms sometimes can get public relations benefits without actually changing the internal culture as a way to enhance external branding by winning awards from third parties as one of the best employers to work at (Dineen & Allen, 2016).

Further, it is sometimes much easier for CEOs at the top to give public statements of good intentions but then internally reward "real metrics," such as meeting aggressive profit goals, to a far greater extent than meeting aggressive gender and diversity hiring and retention goals or culture change objectives – the latter of which may be more challenging and harder to quantify. Moreover, these awards or "top companies" lists can be confusing and misleading to the public because each list often uses different metrics to select the companies, and we do not know which indicators are the most accurate and important. For example, we examined three reputable lists of great workplaces for women in 2018 from Forbes (Valet, 2019), Great Place to Work (Great

Place to Work, n.d.), and Working Mothers (Working Mothers, n.d.). We found little cross-validation, as there was only one company that was listed as one of the top ten in more than one list. Although each list provides information on the metrics used to rank the companies, it is hard to determine which list is more accurate without knowing which indicators in those metrics really represent gender inclusion or equality. The lists may also be biased in favor of larger firms that have the resources to have someone fill out the questionnaire or even self-nominate for the award. Research is needed to develop a way to validate public statements of being a great place to work for women with actual data from employees and managers at all levels of the firm. One practical solution would be to have companies publicly report the gender demography and pay rates at all levels of the firm on their company websites or in an annual report.

- **Increase accountability for advancing gender inclusion through setting measurable goals, transparent reporting, and offering rewards for progress.**

We've noted that espousing good intentions is not enough to ensure change. Setting measurable goals and metrics that hold everyone in the firm accountable for their actions or inactions helps organizations to be more transparent about their progress. Accountability and transparency are cited by experts as two of the most important ingredients of successful diversity and inclusion efforts, such as those of Deloitte (McCracken, 2000), Coca-Cola (Isdell & Bielaszka-DuVernay, 2008), and Lilly (Fitzgerald, 2018). Implementing routine assessment of the multilevel metrics we've recommended above matters. As a chairman of Johnson & Johnson recently stated, "the importance of something is whether you're actually measuring it and you're holding people accountable to improving those numbers" (Zhao, 2019).

In order to increase accountability, many companies are rewarding diversity and inclusion efforts with bonuses. For example, at Microsoft and Intel, 50 percent of executives' cash bonuses are tied to whether they met their diversity and inclusion goals (Zhao, 2019). Ongoing active CEO involvement in setting objectives is also a growing strategy. At Medtronic, a leading high-tech manufacturer of health care equipment, the CEO leads the diversity council and approves aggressive diversity goals for increasing diversity on the board of directors (Johnson, 2017). Medtronic has set global workforce goals to have women make up at least 40 percent of managers by 2020 (Johnson, 2017).

Lastly, another effective way to foster accountability and ensure active CEO involvement is to have the top diversity and inclusion executive report to the CEO, as Dartmouth professor Ella Bell recommends (Ascend, 2019). This ensures that diversity and inclusion issues are directly being communicated to the top of the firm and can more easily be integrated into organizational strategies.

Possible caveats. Research is needed to identify the pros and cons of different types of incentives for D&I goals. For example, companies may focus on meeting short-term metrics such as hiring for diversity rather than retaining diversity or changing the diversity climate (Kossek & Zonia, 1993). Such an approach could backfire, leading to a revolving door for women and stagnant gender representation and gaps at mid-level ranks of the firm. Further studies are needed on the conditions under which metrics and quotas could backfire and lead to a lack of culture change. We've noted that diversity and inclusion efforts have to target multiple levels and many aspects of the organization, and goals and measurement need to be extensive and multifaceted to capture the change. That is why diversity task forces often yield better results than any other narrow-focused program (Dobbin & Kalev, 2016). More research on comparing the effectiveness of different diversity and inclusion programs or rewards and change approaches is needed to promote evidence-based diversity and inclusion practices. For example, research might look at the benefits of adopting change strategies such as mentoring or bias training at the same time that aggressive metrics are adopted and organizational leaders increase attention and rewards related to diversity goals.

- **Acknowledge the pervasiveness of the institutionalized gender bias in employment settings and take actions to remedy it.**

Throughout this book, we have seen numerous examples of institutional implicit bias working against women, from recruitment to performance appraisals to promotion. Organizations can begin by questioning stereotypes and assumptions that get in the way of women's learning and leading, as well as by being open to identifying factors, unintended or not, that may be contributing to women's achievement gaps (Novotney, 2019).

Organization-wide change initiatives customized to a firm's culture with specific relevant examples can be a helpful first step to combat implicit bias by helping employees understand how to recognize and address implicit and explicit bias in HR and organizational systems, and by recommending remedial actions they can take (McCracken, 2000). Such actions can include implicit bias training to reduce stereotyping in interpersonal interactions, but should not stop there. Rather, to be most effective, training and resocializing of new initiatives should be implemented concomitantly with formal changes to reduce institutionalized gender bias in the HR systems – from recruitment, performance evaluation, and pay to promotion processes. Examples of progressive actions include blinding some personal information during the initial recruitment phases (Bertrand & Mullainathan, 2004); not mainly sourcing new hires from referrals from current employees, particularly if the current workforce is not gender or ethnically diverse (Gilbert, 2018); developing a clear candidate and performance evaluation matrix prior to implementation, with multiple appropriately trained raters (Mackenzie et al., 2019); making pay offers based on the position and job experience rather than past salary history (Vagins, n.d.); and openly publicizing pay and promotion criteria and decisions (McCracken, 2000).

Possible caveats. One challenge in eliminating institutionalized biases in the internal culture is that the external labor market is rapidly changing, and employees are working with an employer for shortened employment cycles. The era of the paternalistic employer who adopts a psychological contract of caring for an employee over their career is becoming increasingly outdated and tenuous. Thus, it may not be possible to conduct a "brownfield" type of change in an existing firm. A "brownfield" approach refers to starting a project based on existing systems, which means working with and overcoming existing limitations and constraints (Hoffman, 2017). Rather, it may be better to design firms from the ground up – in a start-up greenfield organizational model of starting from scratch (Hoffman, 2017) – establishing the type of gender-inclusive environment that fits with corporate strategy and mission. As part of the business strategy, organizations may want to do a reset and develop an organizational strategy for managing gender inclusion and diversity (Kossek & Lobel, 1996) and design prototypical new employment practices rather than tinker piecemeal with an existing culture that is not working very well.

Conclusions

We hope that this book will contribute to creating gender-inclusive organizations by starting conversations within organizations; across organizations; between employees, peers, and leaders; between researchers; and between researchers and organizational practitioners. We also hope this book will be useful to students of diversity and inclusion and will promote open dialogue in educational settings as well. Most importantly, we hope that you will be motivated to act to improve gender inclusion in your own backyard – in your daily interactions, your workplaces, and your research and practice. As Professor Debra Meyerson (2001) once said in her research on "tempered radicals," small changes can often start a path toward larger change. May each of the readers of this book be a "tempered radical" on the path toward enhancing women's inclusion and equality at work and in society more generally.

REFERENCES

Allen, T.D., Finkelstein, L.M., & Poteet, M.L. (2009). *Designing workplace mentoring programs: An evidence-based approach.* Oxford: Wiley & Sons.

Amabile, T.M., Patterson, C., Mueller, J., Wojcik, T., Odomirok, P.W., Marsh, M., & Kramer, S.J. (2001). Academic-practitioner collaboration in management research: A case of cross-profession collaboration. *Academy of Management Journal, 44*(2), 418–31. https://doi.org/10.5465/3069464.

Ankrah, S., & AL-Tabbaa, O. (2015). Universities–industry collaboration: A systematic review. *Scandinavian Journal of Management, 31*(3), 387–408. https://doi.org/10.1016/j.scaman.2015.02.003.

Ascend.com. (2019). Summit. Retrieved from https://ascendcommitment .com/2019videos/.

Babcock, P. (2009, 13 April). Diversity accountability requires more than numbers. Retrieved 21 August 2019, from SHRM website: https:// www.shrm.org/resourcesandtools/hr-topics/behavioral-competencies /global-and-cultural-effectiveness/pages/morethannumbers.aspx.

Bach, D. (2016, 12 October). Why do some STEM fields have fewer women than others? UW study may have the answer. Retrieved from https:// www.washington.edu/news/2016/10/12/why-do-some-stem-fields -have-fewer-women-than-others-uw-study-may-have-the-answer/.

Batson, C.D., Polycarpou, M.P., Harmon-Jones, E., Imhoff, H.J., Mitchener, E.C., Bednar, L.L., et al. (1997). Empathy and attitudes: Can feeling for a member of a stigmatized group improve feelings toward the group? *Journal of Personality and Social Psychology, 72*(1), 105–18. https://doi .org/10.1037/0022-3514.72.1.105.

Bertrand, M., & Mullainathan, S. (2004). Are Emily and Greg more employable than Lakisha and Jamal? A field experiment on labor market discrimination. *The American Economic Review, 94*(4), 991–1013. https://doi.org/10.1257/0002828042002561.

Bilimoria, D. (2019, 19 August). Personal communication.

Burke, S.E., Dovidio, J.F., Przedworski, J.M., Hardeman, R.R., Perry, S.P., Phelan, S.M., et al. (2015). Do contact and empathy mitigate bias against gay and lesbian people among heterosexual first-year medical students? A report from the medical student CHANGE study. *Academic Medicine, 90*(5), 645–51. https://doi.org/10.1097/ACM .0000000000000661.

Clancy, K., Lee, K., Rodgers, E., & Richey, C. (2017). Double jeopardy in astronomy and planetary science: Women of color face greater risks of gendered and racial harassment. *Journal of Geophysical Research: Planets, 122*(7), 1610–23. https://doi.org/10.1002/2017JE005256.

Diekman, A.B., Brown, E.R., Johnston, A.M., & Clark, E.K. (2010). Seeking congruity between goals and roles: A new look at why women opt out of science, technology, engineering, and mathematics careers. *Psychological Science, 21*(8), 1051–7. https://doi.org/10.1177 /0956797610377342.

Diekman, A.B., & Eagly, A.H. (2008). *Of men, women, and motivation.* New York: Guilford.

Dineen, B.R., & Allen, D.G. (2016). Third party employment branding: Human capital inflows and outflows following "Best Places to Work" certifications. *Academy of Management Journal, 59*(1), 90–112. https://doi .org/10.5465/amj.2013.1091.

Dobbin, F., & Kalev, A. (2016). Why diversity efforts fail. *Harvard Business Review, 21.* Retrieved from https://hbr.org/2016/07/why-diversity -programs-fail.

Duguid, M.M., & Thomas-Hunt, M.C. (2015). Condoning stereotyping? How awareness of stereotyping prevalence impacts expression of stereotypes. *Journal of Applied Psychology, 100*(2), 343–59. https://doi.org/10.1037 /a0037908.

Eagly, A.H., & Karau, S.J. (2002). Role congruity theory of prejudice toward female leaders. *Psychological Review, 109*(3), 573–98. https://doi .org/10.1037/0033-295X.109.3.573.

Eby, L.T., Lockwood, A.L., & Butts, M. (2006). Perceived support for mentoring: A multiple perspectives approach. *Journal of Vocational Behavior, 68*(2), 267–91. https://doi.org/10.1016/j.jvb.2005.07.003.

Eddleston, K.A., & Powell, G.N. (2008). The role of gender identity in explaining sex differences in business owners' career satisfier preferences.

Journal of Business Venturing, 23(2), 244–56. https://doi.org/10.1016/j.jbusvent.2006.11.002.

Ely, R. (1994). The effects of organizational demographics and social identity on relationships among professional women. *Administrative Science Quarterly, 39*(2), 203–38. https://doi.org/10.2307/2393234.

Emerson, J. (2017, 28 April). Don't give up on unconscious bias training – Make it better. *Harvard Business Review*. Retrieved from https://hbr.org/2017/04/dont-give-up-on-unconscious-bias-training-make-it-better.

Fitzgerald, J. (2018, October). How Lilly is getting more women into leadership positions. *Harvard Business Review*. Retrieved from https://hbr.org/2018/10/how-lilly-is-getting-more-women-into-leadership-positions.

Ghosh, R. (2014). Antecedents of mentoring support: A meta-analysis of individual, relational, and structural or organizational factors. *Journal of Vocational Behavior, 84*(3), 367–84. https://doi.org/10.1016/j.jvb.2014.02.009.

Gilbert, J.C. (2018, 18 September). I'm complicit to institutional bias, here's what I'm doing about it. Retrieved 3 June 2019, from https://www.forbes.com/sites/jaycoengilbert/2018/09/18/im-complicit-to-institutional-bias-heres-what-im-doing-about-it/#29153a5762fa.

Goldin C., & Katz, L.F. (2018). *Women working longer: Increased employment at older ages*. Chicago: University of Chicago Press.

Great Place to Work. (n.d.). Best workplaces for women™ 2018. Retrieved from https://www.greatplacetowork.com/best-workplaces/women/2018.

Helms, M.M., Arfken, D.E., & Bellar, S. (2016). The importance of mentoring and sponsorship in women's career development. *S.A.M. Advanced Management Journal, 81*(3), 4–16. Retrieved from https://search.proquest.com/docview/1833936685?accountid=13360.

Hoffman, A. (2017). Breaking ground: Method and the brownfield vs. greenfield debate. (No. W05C08). William Davidson Institute at the University of Michigan.

Isdell, N., & Bielaszka-DuVernay, C. (2008). How Coca-Cola built strength on diversity. *Harvard Management Update*, U08048.

Johnson, S.K. (2017, 17 August). What 11 CEOs have learned about championing diversity. *Harvard Business Review*. Retrieved from https://hbr.org/2017/08/what-11-ceos-have-learned-about -championing-diversity.

Konrad, A.M., & Linnehan, F. (1995). Formalized HRM structures: Coordinating equal employment opportunity or concealing organizational practices? *Academy of Management Journal*, *38*(3), 787–820. https://doi.org/10.5465/256746.

Kossek, E.E. (2006). Work and family in America: Growing tensions between employment policy and a changing workforce. In E. Lawler & J. O'Toole (Eds.), *America at work: Choices and challenges*, 53–72. New York: Palgrave MacMillan.

Kossek, E.E. (2016, 28 February). Organizer. Opening panel: Career agility: Making it work advice from the experts on career observations. Leadership Excellence and Gender in Organizations Conference, Krannert School of Management and Susan Bulkeley Butler Center for Leadership Excellence at Purdue University. West Lafayette, IN.

Kossek, E.E. (2019, 24 June). Now is the time to move the needle on US work-family policies. *Brink*. Retrieved 19 August 2019 from https:// www.brinknews.com/now-is-the-time-to-move-the-needle -on-u-s-work-family-policies/.

Kossek, E.E., & Lobel, S. (Eds.). (1996). *Managing diversity: Human resource strategies for transforming the workplace*. Cambridge, MA: Blackwell.

Kossek, E.E., Su, R., & Wu, L. (2017). "Opting out" or "pushed out"? Integrating perspectives on women's career equality for gender inclusion and interventions. *Journal of Management*, *43*(1), 228–54. https://doi.org/10.1177/0149206316671582.

Kossek, E.E., & Zonia, S. (1993). Assessing diversity climate: A field study of reactions to employer efforts to promote diversity. *Journal of Organizational Behavior*, *14*(1), 61–81. https://doi.org/10.1002 /job.4030140107.

Lubin, J.S. (2016, 21 June). Companies try a new strategy: Empathy training. *The Wall Street Journal*. Retrieved from https://www.wsj.com /articles/companies-try-a-new-strategy-empathy-1466501403.

Mackenzie, L., Wehner, J., & Correll, S. (2019, 11 January). Why most performance evaluations are biased, and how to fix them. *Harvard Business Review*. Retrieved from https://hbr.org/2019/01/why -most-performance-evaluations-are-biased-and-how-to-fix-them.

McCracken, D.M. (2000). Winning the talent war for women: Sometimes it takes a revolution. *Harvard Business Review*, November–December, 159–64. Retrieved from https://hbr.org/2000/11/winning-the -talent-war-for-women-sometimes-it-takes-a-revolution.

Mejia, Z. (2018, 21 May). Just 24 female CEOs lead the companies on the 2018 Fortune 5000 – fewer than last year. Retrieved from https://www .cnbc.com/2018/05/21/2018s-fortune-500-companies-have-just-24 -female-ceos.html.

Meyerson, D. (2001). *Tempered radicals: How people use difference to inspire change at work*. Boston: Harvard Business School.

Novotney, A. (2019). Renewing the push for equality. *Monitor on Psychology*, *50*, 36–44.

Nye, C.D., Su, R., Rounds, J., & Drasgow, F. (2012). Vocational interests and performance: A quantitative summary of over 60 years of research. *Perspectives on Psychological Science*, *7*, 384–403. https://doi.org/10.1177 /1745691612449021.

Park, T.-Y., Lee, E.-S., & Budd, J.W. (2019). What do unions do for mothers? Paid maternity leave use and the multifaceted roles of labor unions. *ILR Review*, *72*(3), 662–92. https://doi.org/10.1177 /0019793918820032.

Pfeffer, J., & Sutton, R.I. (2000). *The knowing-doing gap: How smart companies turn knowledge into action*. Boston: Harvard Business School Press.

PwC. (2013). PwC's NextGen: A global generational study. Retrieved from https://www.pwc.com/gx/en/hr-management-services/pdf/pwc -nextgen-study-2013.pdf.

Roberson, Q.M. (2006). Disentangling the meanings of diversity and inclusion in organizations. *Group & Organization Management, 31*(2), 212–36. https://doi.org/10.1177/1059601104273064.

Shore, L.M., Cleveland, J.N., & Sanchez, D. (2018). Inclusive workplaces: A review and model. *Human Resource Management Review, 28*(2), 176–89. https://doi.org/10.1016/j.hrmr.2017.07.003.

Todd, A.R., Bodenhausen, G.V., Richeson, J.A., & Galinsky, A.D. (2011). Perspective taking combats automatic expressions of racial bias. *Journal of Personality and Social Psychology, 100*(6), 1027–1142. https://doi.org/10.1037/a0022308.

Vagins, D.J. (n.d.). The simple truth about the gender pay gap. Retrieved from https://www.aauw.org/research/the-simple-truth-about-the-gender-pay-gap/.

Valet, V. (2019, 2 July). America's best employers for women. *Forbes.* Retrieved from https://www.greatplacetowork.com/best-workplaces/women/2018.

Working Mothers. (n.d.). 2018 working mother 100 best companies. Retrieved from https://www.workingmother.com/working-mother-100-best-companies-winners-2018.

Zaki, J. (2019). Making empathy central to your company culture. *Harvard Business Review.* Retrieved from https://hbr.org/2019/05/making-empathy-central-to-your-company-culture.

Zhao, J. (2019, 7 March). These companies are tying executive bonuses to diversity goals. Retrieved 3 June 2019, from PayScale website: https://www.payscale.com/compensation-today/2019/03/tie-bonuses-to-diversity-goals.

ACKNOWLEDGMENTS

This book grew out of the 2016 inaugural conference on gender and leadership excellence and women's career equality held at Purdue University. It planted the seeds to grow into the bi-annual research-to-practice conference series on gender and leadership. This book could not have happened without the support and vision of Jennifer DiDomenico, who is the editor of business and economics at the University of Toronto Press. Writing and editing a book from conference materials is not an easy task; it required much revision and additional research. We deeply appreciated Jennifer's careful and detailed feedback and supportive coaching along the way to bring the book to fruition.

The 2016 conference, which provided the seminal content for the book's foundation, could not have happened without the support of Purdue University's Provost's Office and many sponsors and the hard work of many people. We would like to thank our Purdue University sponsors: the Krannert School of Management and Dean David Hummels; the Krannert School of Management's Women in Management Center led by the associate dean of undergraduate programs, Charlene Sullivan; the Susan Bulkeley Butler Center for Leadership Excellence and its then director, Patrice Buzzanell; ADVANCE Purdue and its director, Christie Sahley;

the Certificate in Entrepreneurship and Innovation Program and its director, Nathalie Duval-Couetil; the Military Family Research Institute and the Center for Families and their director, Shelley MacDermid Wadsworth; the Center for Research on Diversity and Inclusion and its then director, Valeria Sinclair-Chapman; the Women's Gender and Sexuality Studies and its then director, T.J. Boisseau. The contribution from the Land of Lakes Corporation was also critical.

The Purdue University organizing team was essential to the success of the material for this book. We thank Sherry Fisher for her excellence in leading the administrative team in managing all the details to bring the content in this book together as an outgrowth of her managing of the conference. We also thank other members of the planning team: former Purdue graduate students Briana Sotelo and Philip Lemperle; Tim Newton, director of external relations and communications at Krannert School of Management, and his team, including Kristopher Knotts, Jeremy Lwande, and Mike Carmin, who helped us with publicizing the conference and videotaping interviews and sessions; and Ethan Kingery at Purdue Conferences. We thank Marcy Wilhelm-South and Katherine Purple of Purdue University Press for helping us with managing public information releases for dissemination and work-in-progress sessions.

Finally, we would like to thank the wonderful speakers, discussants, and attendees who traveled to the Purdue campus to share their knowledge on gender, diversity, and inclusion. Gathering such a great group of experts together, contributors who were committed to mutual learning and dialogue, created a rich educational community and stimulated meaningful, in-depth content for this book, which we hope will help advance understanding of gender inclusion in society.

Dr Ellen Ernst Kossek
Basil S. Turner Professor of Management and Research Director,
Susan Bulkeley Butler Center for Leadership Excellence

Dr Kyung-Hee Lee
Research Scholar, Susan Bulkeley Butler Center for Leadership
Excellence and Krannert School of Management

Purdue University
West Lafayette, Indiana
22 November 2019

ABOUT THE EDITORS

Ellen Ernst Kossek (PhD Yale University), the Basil S. Turner Professor at Purdue University's Krannert School of Management and research director of the Susan Bulkeley Butler Center for Leadership Excellence, is the first elected president of the Work-Family Researchers Network. She is a fellow in the Academy of Management, American Psychological Association, and the Society of Industrial-Organizational Psychology. Her award-winning research examines transforming gender and work-family life organizational practices such as new trends toward implementing gender inclusion and flexibility. She has won a Work-Life Legacy award from the Families and Work Institute for helping to build or advance the work-life movement. She has won or been a finalist multiple times within the last decade for the Rosabeth Moss Kanter work-family research excellence award recognizing the best work-family paper published in a given year among several thousand published across disciplines. Dr Kossek has also won the Academy of Management's Gender and Diversity in Organizations Sage Award for Scholarly Contributions for advancing the understanding of gender and diversity in organizations. Prior to joining Purdue, Dr Kossek was University Distinguished Professor at Michigan State University. Before her academic career, she worked on human resource issues for major corporations in the United States, Asia, and Europe. Her research has been funded by the National Institutes of Health, the National Science Foundation, the Alfred P. Sloan Foundation, the Russell Sage Foundation, and the Gerber Foundation, among others. Her research has appeared in top academic journals as well as on National Public Radio and CNN and in the *Financial Times*, *Time* magazine, the *Washington Post*, the *Harvard Business Review*, the *Chicago Tribune*, *Forbes*, and the *Wall Street Journal*. She has been invited to speak on work-family issues to business, government, and educational organizations in more than fifteen countries around the globe.

Kyung-Hee Lee is a research scholar at the Krannert School of Management and the Susan Bulkeley Butler Center at Purdue University. She earned her PhD at Texas Tech and previously worked as a postdoctoral research associate at the Military Family Research Institute at Purdue University and Virginia Tech. Her research interests include work-family issues and work-family–related online training, military families, dyadic and longitudinal processes of intimate relationships and voluntary childlessness.

CONTRIBUTORS

Diana Bilimoria is the KeyBank Professor and chair of the Department of Organizational Behavior at the Weatherhead School of Management, Case Western Reserve University. Dr Bilimoria's research focuses on gender, diversity, and inclusion in leadership and governance, and organizational transformation. She is the author of several books and has published extensively in leading journals and edited volumes. She was the division chair of the Gender and Diversity in Organizations Division of the Academy of Management and has served as the editor of the *Journal of Management Education*. Dr Bilimoria has been internationally recognized for her leadership, research, and service. At Case Western Reserve University she received the Flora Stone Mather Center for Women's Spotlight Series Prize for Women's Scholarship and the Weatherhead School of Management's MBA and Doctoral Teaching Excellence Awards. She received her PhD in business administration from the University of Michigan.

Nellie Borrero is the managing director of global inclusion and diversity at Accenture. Nellie joined Accenture in 1986. She created the first role for diversity efforts and is embraced as a beloved and deeply committed advocate for change for women, for minorities, and for people. Nellie holds a crucial leadership role and is a driving force behind the company's diversity initiatives. The most recent innovations under Nellie's leadership include the creation of a development program for high-performing women globally; the design of career progression initiatives for women; global positioning of the LGBT and persons with disability agenda; as well as the design and execution of ethnic diversity programs. Nellie is married and has a daughter and son. She enjoys her family life, reading, playing tennis, and purposefully giving to the world.

Patrice M. Buzzanell is an emeritus professor in the Brian Lamb School of Communication and was the Susan Bulkeley Butler Chair for Leadership Excellence and director of the Butler Center at Purdue University at the time of the conference. Currently, Dr Buzzanell is the chair and professor of communication at the University of South Florida. Dr Buzzanell's research focuses on the intersections of career, leadership, gender, and resilience. Specifically, she focuses on the everyday negotiations, policies, and structures that produce and are produced by the intersections. Dr Buzzanell has been honored nationally and internationally with the 2014 Velux Faculty Research Fellowship from Copenhagen Business School and the B. Aubrey Fisher Mentorship Award from the International Communication Association (ICA) in 2016. As well she is an ICA fellow (2011), and an endowed visiting professor, School of Media and Design, at Shanghai Jiaotong University. In 2010, she was honored to deliver the NCA Carroll C. Arnold Distinguished Lecture, "Seduction and Sustainability: The Politics of Feminist Communication and Career Scholarship," documenting the need for change in institutions of higher education and posing possibilities for greater inclusion. Dr Buzzanell received her PhD in communication from Purdue University.

Anne Donovan is the U.S. and West cluster transformation leader for human capital at PricewaterhouseCoopers (PwC), responsible for human capital strategy and innovation leading culture change through a variety of initiatives related to the work environment, such as work-life flexibility, the business model, and workforce demographics. Anne's deep knowledge of human capital issues draws upon her thirty years of experience at PwC, where she has held diverse roles across client service, operations, diversity, and firm strategy. Anne also has strong expertise in operational effectiveness and in engaging and supporting the firm and its people in leading positive change. A 1983 graduate of California State University, Northridge, with a BS in accountancy, Anne resides in Los Angeles with her twin girls, Grace and Kathryn.

Nathalie Duval-Couetil is the director of the Certificate in Entrepreneurship and Innovation Program, associate director of the Burton D. Morgan Center, and an associate professor in the Department of Technology, Leadership, and Innovation at Purdue University. She is responsible for the launch and development of the university's multidisciplinary undergraduate entrepreneurship program, which has involved 1,800 students each year. Prior to her work in academia, Nathalie spent several years in the field of market research and business strategy consulting in Europe and the United States with Booz Allen Hamilton and Data and Strategies Group. She currently serves on the board of the United States Association for Small Business and Entrepreneurship. She received her MBA from Babson College and a PhD from Purdue University.

Kimberly Eddleston is the Schulze Distinguished Professor of entrepreneurship and innovation at Northeastern University. Professor Eddleston received her PhD from the University of Connecticut and her graduate degree from Cornell University and Group ESSEC (IMHI). Professor Eddleston is widely published in the field of entrepreneurship. She has won multiple awards for her research on family businesses as well as women entrepreneurs and managers. She is an associate editor of the *Journal of Business Venturing* and serves on the editorial board of multiple journals, including *Entrepreneurship Theory and Practice, Family Business Review, Journal of Family Business Strategy*, and *Strategic Entrepreneurship Journal*. Professor Eddleston has helped many students successfully join their family's firms and has also assisted students in the launch of their own enterprises. She has also developed a small business consulting project curriculum that has helped more than 150 businesses and has been featured at several entrepreneurship conferences and in *Inc. Magazine*.

David Hummels is the Dr Samuel R. Allen Dean of the Krannert School of Management and Distinguished Professor of economics at Purdue University. In his faculty life, Professor Hummels teaches courses in international economics and has won multiple teaching awards at the graduate and undergraduate level. His research focuses on a broad range of issues in international trade, including offshoring, product differentiation, barriers to trade, and the broader impacts of aviation, infrastructure, and trade facilitation on trade and economic development. He has published four books and more than forty research articles in major economic journals including *American Economic Review*, the *Journal of Political Economy*, the *Quarterly Journal of Economics*, the *Review of Economics and Statistics*, the *Journal of International Economics*, and the *Journal of Economic Perspectives*. Professor Hummels is a research associate of the National Bureau of Economic Research, an associate editor of the *Journal of International Economics*, and an associate director of the Forum for Research on Empirical International Trade. He has worked as a consultant for and visiting scholar at a wide variety of central banks, development banks, and policy institutes around the world. He previously served on the faculty of the University of Chicago's Booth School of Business.

Charlice Hurst is an assistant professor of management and organization at Mendoza College of Business, University of Notre Dame. The primary focus of her research is on the roles of self-concept, gender, and race in interpersonal dynamics in the workplace and how interpersonal relationships influence well-being and performance. Prior to embarking on her academic career, she spent ten years as a fundraising and management consultant to non-profit organizations and social enterprises. She received her PhD in management from the University of Florida and her International MBA in economics from the University of South Carolina.

Beth A. Livingston is an assistant professor, Department of Management and Organizations, at Tippie College of Business, University of Iowa. Her research covers three overlapping areas of interest: gender and diversity, stereotyping/stigma/discrimination, and the management of work and family. Dr Livingston earned her PhD in management and organizational behavior from the University of Florida. She has received the Robert N. Stern Award for Teaching and Mentoring at Cornell University.

Denise Lewin Loyd is an associate professor of business administration at University of Illinois at Urbana-Champaign. Her work on diversity in teams examines how group composition affects reactions to similar and dissimilar others and impacts individual and team outcomes. Professor Loyd earned her PhD in management and organizations from Northwestern University's Kellogg School of Management. She has received awards for her research from the International Association for Conflict Management, the Academy of Management, and the State Farm Foundation.

Kelly Mack is the vice-president for undergraduate STEM education and executive director of Project Kaleidoscope, a non-profit organization focusing on undergraduate STEM education reform, at the Association of American Colleges and Universities (AAC&U). Prior to joining the AAC&U, Dr Mack was the senior program director for the National Science Foundation (NSF) ADVANCE

Program while on loan from the University of Maryland Eastern Shore (UMES) where, as a professor of biology, she taught courses in physiology and endocrinology for seventeen years. Dr Mack earned a BS degree in biology from UMES and, later, a PhD degree in physiology from Howard University. She has had extensive training and experience in the area of cancer research, with her research efforts focusing primarily on the use of novel anti-tumor agents in breast tumor cells. Most recently, her research focus has involved the use of bioflavonoids in the regulation of oestrogen receptor positive (ER+) and oestrogen receptor negative (ER-) breast-tumor cell proliferation.

Mariana Monteiro is currently the director of diversity and inclusion at Otis Elevator Co. She was the global ombudsman and executive counsel for GE (General Electric) Power Business. For sixteen years, she held human resources generalist and specialist roles with increased responsibility and global coverage across multiple GE segments and industries. She has ample experience in all aspects of human resources operations, from mergers and acquisitions to talent recruitment and assessment, and from executive coaching to union negotiations. Mariana has also worked as a financial analyst and is a certified black belt in martial arts. Prior to her work at GE, Mariana was a prosecutor in Buenos Aires State; she has practiced law in her native country, Argentina – specializing in civil and employment law – and has taught philosophy and civil law at the University of La Plata Law School, Buenos Aires.

Lisa Nishii is an associate professor of human resource studies at the Industrial and Labor Relations (ILR) School and vice-provost for undergraduate education at Cornell University. Dr Nishii is an expert on inclusion in organizations. Her research focuses on the combined influence of organizational practices, leadership behaviors, and climate for inclusion on individual and group-level outcomes.

Nishii actively publishes in top-tier journals, including *Academy of Management Review, Academy of Management Journal, Journal of Applied Psychology, Personnel Psychology,* and *Science.* She serves on a variety of college and university-level councils for diversity, globalization, and engaged learning. Dr Nishii also consults with multinational companies, primarily on matters related to diversity and inclusion and organizational assessment. She received a PhD and an MA in organizational psychology from the University of Maryland, and a BA in economics from Wellesley College.

Alyssa Panitch has been professor and vice-provost at Purdue University. Currently, she is the Edward Teller Professor and department chair of the Department of Biomedical Engineering at the University of California-Davis. Professor Panitch has received the National Science Foundation Career Award and has been a Purdue Faculty Scholar. She served on the biomaterials and biointerfaces study section for the National Institutes of Health from 2008 to 2012, and in 2011 she was elected to the American Institute for Medical and Biological Engineers' College of Fellows. She has been on the editorial advisory board for *Biomacromolecules* since 2004 and on the editorial board of *Biomatter* since 2010, and is an associate editor for *Cellular and Molecular Bioengineering.* She earned bachelor's degrees in chemical engineering from the University of Massachusetts at Amherst and in biochemistry from Smith College. She completed her doctorate at the University of Massachusetts at Amherst.

Belle Rose Ragins is the Sheldon B. Lubar Professor of Management at the University of Wisconsin-Milwaukee. Her research interests focus on mentoring, diversity, and positive relationships at work. Her current research examines the positive impact of mentoring on employees' organizational attachment and the role of gender and diversity in these relationships. She has also researched the glass ceiling, sexual harassment, racism at work, and sexual orientation in organizations. Dr Ragins has received a number of national awards for her research, including the Sage Life-Time Achievement Award for Scholarly Contributions to Management, the Academy of Management Mentoring Legacy Award, the ASTD Research Award, the Saroj Parasuraman Best Publication Award, and the Center for Creative Leadership's Walter F. Ulmer Applied Research Award for lifetime scholarly achievements. Dr Ragins is an invited member of the Society for Organizational Behavior, a Fulbright Senior Specialist Scholar, and a fellow of the Academy of Management (AOM), the Society for Industrial-Organizational Psychology (SIOP), the American Psychological Society (APS), the Society for the Psychology of Women (SPW), and the American Psychological Association (APA). She is the current editor of the *Academy of Management Review*.

Christie Sahley is a professor of biology, Associate Head and Office of the Provost, and director of the Center for Faculty Success at Purdue University. Dr Sahley has been active as a scholar for more than twenty-five years, contributing to the literature in the areas of the behavioral and cellular analysis of learning and memory. Her research focuses on associative learning, the way in which casual relationships are extracted from the environment and allow animals to modify their behavior on the basis of learned associations between cues and consequences. Dr Sahley currently is lead co-principal investigator (Co-PI) for the Purdue ADVANCE initiative. She is director of the ADVANCE-Purdue Center for Faculty Success and special advisor to the provost for gender equity.

Nina Swanson has been working in organization development, talent, and learning for more than twenty years. She is currently the talent strategy lead for Walmart's eCommerce and Technology segment, where she leads all organizational development, change management, and talent management efforts. Prior to Walmart, she was with eBay/PayPal for more than eleven years, where she held a variety of roles in the learning and organization development (L&OD) function; these roles included L&OD partner to the largest business unit in PayPal (Global CS & Ops); global initiative lead to improve people manager effectiveness across eBay Inc.; and leading efforts to support the eBay/PayPal separation and ensure the continuation of core people processes during the transition. Nina has also led global teams across several industries, including financial services, health care, and professional services. Nina earned a BA in psychology from St Olaf College in Northfield, Minnesota, and a master's degree in labor and industrial relations from Michigan State University. She lives in Omaha, Nebraska, with her husband, two children, and Scout (the dog). When not at work, she enjoys cooking from her husband's gardens and time on the lake at her cabin in northern Wisconsin.

Orlando Taylor is vice-president for strategic initiatives and research at Fielding Graduate University, Santa Barbara, California, and director of its Marie Fielder Center for Democracy, Leadership, and Education. He is also a Distinguished Fellow of the Association of American Colleges and Universities (AACU) and a professor in Fielding's School of Leadership Studies. Dr Taylor has been a national leader for many years on issues pertaining to diversity and inclusion in higher education. He has been a particularly vigorous advocate and spokesperson on topics and issues relating to access and equity in higher education and to preparing the next generation of researchers, as well as faculty members, for the nation's colleges and universities. Dr Taylor received a PhD degree from the University of Michigan and has been a recipient of that university's distinguished alumni award. He is a fellow of and recipient of honors from the American Speech-Language-Hearing Association. He received his undergraduate degree from Hampton University and a master's degree from Indiana University. He has been awarded honorary doctorate degrees from Purdue University,

Indiana University, The Ohio State University, Hope College, De-
Pauw University, Denison University, and Southern Connecticut
State University.

Rosalia Thomas is the worldwide director of diversity and inclusion (D&I) at IBM. Her team is responsible for the development of
diversity, inclusion, cultural competency, and work-life strategies
that fully align with IBM's business strategies. Rosalia is an experienced human resources professional with twenty years in the HR
field. Previously she was human resources director for her company's United States East operations. Rosalia is a founding board
member of the Women's Executive Committee for Habitat for Hu-
manity. She is a member of Leadership Cobb and is on the board
at St Joseph's Hospital. She has served on the board of Center for
Puppetry Arts, Georgia Campaign for Adolescent Pregnancy Pre-
vention, and Kennesaw University Coles College Executive MBA
Program. She graduated from Mercer University with a degree in
management and marketing and has an MBA from the same university. She is Cuban born, married, and has a son, Christopher, who is
the pride of her life.